Cross-Media Ownership and Democratic Practice in Canada

Cross-Media Ownership and Democratic Practice in Canada

Content-Sharing and the Impact of New Media

Walter C. Soderlund
Colette Brin
Lydia Miljan
Kai Hildebrandt

 The University of Alberta Press

Published by
The University of Alberta Press
Ring House 2
Edmonton, Alberta, Canada T6G 2E1
www.uap.ualberta.ca

Copyright © 2012 Walter C. Soderlund, Colette Brin,
Lydia Miljan & Kai Hildebrandt

Library and Archives Canada Cataloguing in Publication

   Cross-media ownership and democratic practice in
Canada : content-sharing and the impact of new media / by
Walter C. Soderlund ... [et al.].

Includes bibliographical references and index.
ISBN 978-0-88864-605-7

   1. Canadian newspapers--Ownership. 2. Press monopolies--
Canada. 3. Newspaper publishing--Canada. 4. Broadcasting--
Canada. I. Soderlund, W. C. (Walter C.)

PN4914.O9C76 2012   071'.1   C2011-907437-0

First edition, first printing, 2012.
Printed and bound in Canada by Houghton Boston
Printers, Saskatoon, Saskatchewan.
Copyediting and Proofreading by Kirsten Craven.
Indexing by Elizabeth Macfie.

All rights reserved. No part of this publication may be produced, stored in
a retrieval system, or transmitted in any form or by any means (electronic,
mechanical, photocopying, recording, or otherwise) without prior written
consent. Contact the University of Alberta Press for further details.

The University of Alberta Press is committed to protecting our natural
environment. As part of our efforts, this book is printed on Enviro Paper: it
contains 100% post-consumer recycled fibres and is acid- and chlorine-free.

The University of Alberta Press gratefully acknowledges the support received
for its publishing program from The Canada Council for the Arts. The
University of Alberta Press also gratefully acknowledges the financial support
of the Government of Canada through the Canada Book Fund (CBF) and the
Government of Alberta through the Alberta Multimedia Development Fund
(AMDF) for its publishing activities.

To Walter Romanow and Florian Sauvageau

Contents

ix		Preface
1	1	Media and Democratic Governance

Part I Is Content-Sharing a Consequence of Convergence?

21	2	Convergence: Promises and Problems
41	3	Content-Sharing in National Media
57	4	Content-Sharing in English-Language Local Market Media

Part II Canadian Media: Now and into the Future

67	5	Media Executives Assess the Impact of Convergence and New Media
79	6	Stakeholders Assess the State of Canadian Media
95	7	Old Media, New Media, Any Media?

103	Postscript
109	Notes
119	References
135	Contributors
137	Index

List of Tables

37	TABLE 2.1	National Media Studied
42	TABLE 3.1	Cross-Media Ownership in Canada, as of 2008
43	TABLE 3.2A	Story Lead Similarity, by Test and Control Groups (English)
43	TABLE 3.2B	Story Lead Similarity, by Test and Control Groups (French)
45	TABLE 3.3A	Story Dimension Similarity, by Test and Control Groups (English)
45	TABLE 3.3B	Story Dimension Similarity, by Test and Control Groups (French)
46	TABLE 3.4A	Language Similarity, by Test and Control Groups (English)
46	TABLE 3.4B	Language Similarity, by Test and Control Groups (French)
47	TABLE 3.5A	Source Similarity, by Test and Control Groups (English)
47	TABLE 3.5B	Source Similarity, by Test and Control Groups (French)
48	TABLE 3.6A	Editorial "Spin" Similarity, by Test and Control Groups (English)
48	TABLE 3.6B	Editorial "Spin" Similarity, by Test and Control Groups (French)
49	TABLE 3.7	Editorial "Spin" Similarity, by Individual Media Groups (English)
50	TABLE 3.8A	Index Similarity, by Test and Control Groups (English)
50	TABLE 3.8B	Index Similarity, by Test and Control Groups (French)
58	TABLE 4.1	Story Lead Similarity, by Local Test and Selected Control Groups
58	TABLE 4.2	Story Dimension Similarity, by Local Test and Selected Control Groups
59	TABLE 4.3	Story Language Similarity, by Test and Selected Control Groups
60	TABLE 4.4	Story Source Similarity, by Local Test and Selected Control Groups
61	TABLE 4.5	Story "Spin" Similarity, by Local Test and Selected Control Groups
61	TABLE 4.6	Overall Similarity Index, by Local Test and Selected Control Groups

Preface

THORSTEN QUANDT AND JANE SINGER (2009) have pointed out the difficulties involved in attempting to examine the impact of convergence on mass media through content analysis; namely that the subject has a nasty way of shifting ground very quickly. During the course of our study we came to appreciate the wisdom of their observation.

The research reported in this book began in 2006 as a straightforward attempt to document the amount of content-sharing that had been achieved by three major Canadian media companies (Canwest Global Communications, CTVglobemedia and Quebecor) that in 2000 realized the goal of cross-ownership of major television and newspaper properties. By the time we had analyzed the results of our 2007 content analysis of paired TV and newspaper stories from the above companies and began writing up the findings (presented in Part I of this book), it was clear that the focus of the research had to shift to explaining why convergence had not worked. The purported "synergies" that were clearly anticipated had not materialized, as television and newspapers are clearly (as various people associated with media industries told us) very different animals, reporters have minds of their own, and, in Quebec, a Canadian Radio-television and Telecommunications Commission (CRTC) regulation and restrictive labour contracts stood in the way of any implementation. As it turned out, not only was convergence unsuccessful in "reaggregating" media pieces, the debt incurred by Canwest's venture into cross-ownership arguably led, in 2009, to the bankruptcy of the company and yet another restructuring of the Canadian media landscape in 2010.

By the time we began conducting interviews with media executives in 2009, which had been conceived originally as adding some context to the content analysis findings, we had in fact established a new set of goals. Thus, the interviews now included other media stakeholders, and focused for the most part on reasons why convergence had not worked, and especially where Canadian media industries were headed in the face of competition from "new media" and growing financial challenges brought about by the economic recession. These interviews provide the majority of material that appears in Part II. Our conclusions are that, with the important exception of Quebecor, content-sharing between television and newspapers is passé, and that both media are now preoccupied with developing their own web applications, especially with finding ways to make the Internet profitable.

Many organizations and people are in line for thanks for our being able to do the research for this book, and none is more important than the Social Sciences and Humanities Research Council of Canada (SSHRC), which funded the project under grant 410-2006-0226. Also critical was an earlier financial contribution from Cecil Houston, Dean of the Faculty of Arts and Social Sciences at the University of Windsor, that allowed Colette Brin to travel from Quebec City to Windsor to work on the SSHRC grant application. Also at the University of Windsor, Niharendu Biswas and Ranjana Bird (Acting Vice-President Research and Vice-President Research, respectively, during the period of the study) were always supportive of our efforts, as was Tom Najem, Head of the Political Science Department. At Université Laval we wish to thank especially Andrée Courtmanche, Research Coordinator at Faculté des lettres, for support in developing the project and helpful assistance at different stages of the research; Daniel Giroux, Secretary General of the Centre d'études sur les médias, for insights and constant collaboration; and Ulric Deschênes, Instructor at the Département d'information et de communication, for statistical analysis and various helpful suggestions.

We wish as well to thank our coders and those who helped us with data entry at both the University of Windsor and Université Laval. At Windsor thanks go to John Dubé, Steve Ovens, Andrea Anderson, and Daryl Ann Sdao for coding, and to Grantly Franklin and Daryl Ann Sdao for data entry. At Laval thanks go to Thierry Lavoie, Christelle Paré and Marie-Michèle Sauvageau for data entry and coding; to Olivier Bouchard, for design of the multimedia coding system and ongoing technical support; and to Marie Bédard, Justin Dupuis and Anne-Marie Brunelle for coding.

Of course, special thanks go to all those who agreed to interviews with us. We hope that we have accurately reported the views you shared with us.

Securing the necessary funding and actually carrying out a research study mean little unless the results find their way into the hands of interested readers by way of publication. For this crucial stage of the research we wish to thank Peter Midgley, Senior Editor (Acquisitions) for University of Alberta Press, Kirsten Craven, Copyeditor, and Mary Lou Roy, Production Editor, who oversaw the book's production.

Walter C. Soderlund
Colette Brin
Lydia Miljan
Kai Hildebrandt

1

Media and Democratic Governance

THE START OF THE MILLENNIUM heralded a new age of media concentration in Canada. While for decades the newspaper industry had been engaged in ownership consolidation, these efforts paled in comparison to what began in 2000. In July 2000, Canwest Global Communications Corp., owner of the Global Television network, announced its intention to purchase the majority of newspapers held by Conrad Black's Hollinger Inc. Then in September, Quebecor Inc. and la Caisse de dépôt et de placement du Québec made a public offer to acquire all the outstanding shares of Groupe Vidéotron Ltée, giving Quebecor control of the largest French-language television network in Canada in addition to its extensive English- and French-language newspaper holdings.[1] By November 2000, CTV Inc. had accepted a takeover bid from Bell Canada Enterprises (BCE), which BCE then combined with the Thomson-owned *Globe and Mail* to form Bell Globemedia. Thus, in less than six months' time all three of these companies combined major newspaper, television and Internet properties under one corporate umbrella in the hopes of "reaggregating media fragments" in order to create profit-generating synergies (Goldstein, 2002; also see Pitts, 2002).

This was but the start of moves toward convergence in Canadian media; more was yet to come. Most notably, the December 2005 acquisition by Torstar (the parent company of the *Toronto Star*, Canada's largest circulation daily newspaper) of a 20 per cent ownership stake in Bell Globemedia,[2] owner of the *Globe and Mail* (arguably Canada's most influential newspaper) and CTV (Canada's most watched television network), not only put into play a potential content-creating juggernaut, it left only a handful of major Canadian newspapers not linked by ownership to a television broadcaster: the Halifax *Chronicle-Herald*, the *Winnipeg Free Press* and Power Corporation's *La Presse* and *Le Soleil*,[3] plus *Le Devoir* (Bruser, 2005, Dec. 3).

Convergence, as a function of cross-media ownership, has been portrayed by its critics as a horrendous outcome for both a free press and the democracy it serves. At the same time, it has been seen by its proponents (mainly owners of these media) as the saviour of mass media in an age of "narrowcasting," the impact of "new media," and, perhaps most important of all, diminishing profits.

Most scholars who have addressed the problem see the impact of concentrated media ownership on democratic practice as leading to negative outcomes. Democratic theorists dating back at least as far as John Milton [1608–1674], John Locke [1632–1704], and John Stuart Mill [1806–1873] have looked at the critical relationship between the governed and those who govern. Out of this examination has evolved the proposition underpinning what has become known as the "Libertarian Theory" of the press—that good decisions tend to emerge from situations where there is an abundance of competing information. This in turn has provided the foundation for the classic "free market place of ideas" argument, wherein "good" information is said to prevail over "bad" (see Milton, 1971; Locke, 1965; Mill, 1955). In more recent times, this fundamental argument has been restated time and again (Commission on Freedom of the Press, 1947; Siebert, Peterson and Schramm, 1956; Dahl, 1989; McQuail, 1992; Page, 1996). The following statement from the Declaration of Talloires, adopted by leaders of independent news organizations from twenty countries at the Voices of Freedom conference in 1981, catches the essence of the relationship: "From robust public debate grows better understanding of the issues facing a nation and its peoples; and out of understanding greater chances for solutions" (World Press Freedom Committee, 1981). In the Canadian context, the case has been reiterated in the Standing Senate Committee on Transport and Communications' *Final Report on the Canadian News Media*:

To make informed decisions, citizens need a wide range of news and information. *They also need access to a broad and diverse array of opinions and analysis about matters of public interest.* Journalists are important providers of such information, as are the information media that transmit such material. This is why the freedom of the press is widely recognized as a central pillar of any democracy (Canada, 2006, italics added).

The power of mass media to influence citizen attitudes on questions of public policy, especially those that lie outside individuals' personal experience, has been established first through "agenda-setting" and more recently through "framing" (also referred to as "second level agenda-setting") research. This stream of media-effects research can be traced back to Bernard Cohen's much-quoted phrase that while the press "may not be successful much of the time in telling people what to think,...it is stunningly successful in telling its readers what to think *about*" (1963: 14, italics in the original). In a 1968 study of voter attitudes, Maxwell McCombs and Donald Shaw linked the salience of issues covered in mass media to what voters considered to be important and called this phenomenon *agenda-setting*. In more recent research, Maxwell McCombs and Amy Reynolds assert that "[e]stablishing this salience among the public so that an issue becomes the focus of public attention, and perhaps even action, is the initial stage in the formation of public opinion" (2002: 1), and indeed, over the years the agenda-setting effect has been confirmed in numerous research studies (see for example, Salwen, 1988; Rogers and Dearing, 1988; McCombs and Shaw, 1993; Kosicki, 1993; Weaver, 2007).

However, the power of mass media goes beyond the simple transfer of issue salience. Gadi Wolfsfeld, among others, has pointed out that in the reporting of news events, in addition to the raising of issue salience through repeated coverage over time, there is the phenomenon of *framing*—the interpretations that journalists place on the events they are reporting. Thus, reporting must be seen as a combination of information and interpretation (1997: 31–36). Moreover, in making sense of events for audiences, journalists tend to look for well-understood contexts in which to place breaking news—a prime example being the "communist menace" frame to categorize various left-wing reform movements during the Cold War, and more recently the "War on Terror" frame to explain the US-led invasion of Iraq (for research on framing see Iyengar, 1991; Entman, 1993; Ghanem, 1997; Robinson, 2002; Entman, 2004; Scheufele and Tewksbury, 2007).

The significance of agenda-setting and framing for this study is that ownership, if it has a mind to do so based on concern for profit or ideology, can exert considerable influence not only on what the public considers to be important issues by controlling what "news" actually gets to be "news" (i.e., "gatekeeping"), but on how those issues are presented in terms of dealing with them. And there is no doubt that Canadians have access to a very narrow range of mainstream ownership options from which to glean their information and interpretations.

There is, however, a competing view that holds that some limit on content diversity is not necessarily a bad development for democracy. For example, Karl Deutsch (1954) has pointed out that a community's level of integration can be measured by the amount of "within-group" communication as opposed to "between-group" communication. And, of course, the type of extensive communication leading to the formation and maintenance of a "political community" depends in large part on a people having what are termed *shared experiences* (see Anderson, 1991).

First in a journal article (1995) and later in his widely cited study of civic disengagement in the United States, *Bowling Alone*, Robert Putnam linked media behaviour to what he termed "the erosion of America's social capital" (2000: 217). While stopping short of arguing cause and effect, he noted that "news and entertainment have become increasingly individualized....As late as 1975 Americans nationwide chose among a handful of television programs. Barely a quarter century later, cable, satellite, video, and the Internet provide an exploding array of individual choice" (2000: 216).

Donald Shaw and Bradley Hamm, however, did make an explicit connection between the decline of "mass media" and reduction in a sense of "national community." They argued that the cumulative effect of "newer communication technologies" was that individuals are able increasingly to seek out *personal sources of information*, enabling them:

1. To listen to many sources of information other than those of mass media, which tend to cover the activities of those in power and official sources.
2. To locate other people like themselves....

3. To gather and send information within a socially reinforcing group without suffering pangs of anxiety from separation from the larger community....
4. To participate in special groups that try to influence the larger society...or to withdraw from the larger society with little sense of social loss or obligation—to live in space, rather than a place (Shaw and Hamm, 1997: 222).

In the context of the contemporary Canadian media scene, media analyst Kenneth Goldstein has also challenged the view that having a wide diversity in points of view is necessarily helpful to democracy. He argues specifically that

> [i]n Canada and the US, broadcasting may already have passed its peak as a shaper of our shared experience. While broadcasting will continue to be a major influence on our experience, *the fragmentation of the medium may at the same time be reducing the amount of that experience that is common or shared* (Goldstein, 2004: 14, italics added).

Taking Goldstein's argument a step further, Maria Simone and Jan Fernback make the point that a growing number of information sources may in fact hinder the development of a democratic public sphere:

> fragmentation can result in a series of enclaves, with publics that may fail to engage each other in meaningful deliberation. This situation does little to address the fact that while each public maintains its own shared identity and ideology, the national and international spheres must include each of these publics in ongoing national debate (2006: 302-303).

A *Business Week* editorial agrees, suggesting that niche media outlets tend to reinforce and amplify "preexisting points of view, making compromise—the essence of a working democracy—harder than ever to achieve" (2004, July 12).

Pamela Shoemaker and Stephen Reese (1991) have argued convincingly that media impact stems from the *content* that they disseminate and a wealth of research has established that mass publics rely primarily on media for their information on important issues. In this context, most scholars agree that media play a crucial role in the functioning of representative democracy. However, with the ongoing fragmentation of both mass media audiences and media platforms, is the strategy of convergence—the attempt to "reaggregate the fragments"—necessarily one that will harm democracy in a country such as Canada that is already characterized by significant cultural and regional divisions?

Whatever the case, it is clear that *media ownership convergence*, defined for the purposes of this book as combining television and newspaper properties under one corporate owner, can lead to content-sharing strategies among its different media platforms—in fact, content-sharing is an often stated intention and purpose of convergence. This, in turn, very likely would reduce the overall number of divergent viewpoints available to Canadian citizens as they make decisions regarding political leadership and questions of public policy. We must bear in mind, however, that the relationship between diversity of information and democratic practice is complex, and we cannot assume that more diversity in media content is necessarily a "good" thing. The key issue then revolves around *how much diversity of information is optimal for the reasonable functioning of democracy*, and, as the debate outlined above demonstrates, this is not an easy question to answer. Nevertheless, we submit that an ownership convergence of the magnitude experienced in Canada since 2000 signalled no less than a fundamental transformation in the ownership structure of mass media in the country and that the impact of this change on democratic practices needs to be assessed.

Convergence: Implications for Democratic Practice

In addition to the previously examined debate over how much diversity in views as expressed in mass media is good for democracy, two further arguments in defense of media ownership convergence have been advanced:

- that there are a vast number of media outlets available to Canadians, and
- that media owners are not interested in controlling content.

Let us examine briefly the validity of both these arguments.

Canadians have a large number of media outlets available to them

It has been noted by many media observers that Canadians now have access to more sources of information than ever before; cited in these arguments are the presence of the "new media," especially satellite television and, of course, the ever-growing Internet. Charles Dalfen, then Chair of the Canadian Radio-television and Telecommunications Commission (CRTC), in testimony before the Standing Senate Committee on Transport and Communications, explained that "in practically every medium, you will find that there are a larger number of owners and a larger number of broadcasting and newspaper outlets over...[the]...10-year period [1991–2001]" (Canada, 2004: 66). Of course, Canadians are not restricted to their own media; as Kenneth Goldstein has noted, the number of Canadians registered with the *New York Times* website, nytimes.com, exceeded "the average daily circulation of any daily newspaper in Canada" (2002: 3). As a result, primarily due to the growth of these new sources of information, *National Post* columnist Marni Soupcoff did not see ownership convergence as problematic: "*When one looks at the media as a whole (cable and satellite television, radio, daily newspapers, weekly newspapers, Internet sites, web-based newsletters), there are more voices available to Canadian consumers than ever before*" (Soupcoff, 2003, Oct. 8, italics in the original).

Not all observers, however, are convinced by this line of argument. Robert McChesney, writing about the media situation in the United States, specifically argued that ownership convergence works to nullify the myriad of voices that might be seen to be resulting from the addition of new media outlets. He pointed out that "[m]erely being able to launch a website is not sufficient to contend with the enormous market advantage of the media giants as they colonize the Internet" (2000: xxii). In the Canadian context, David Taras claimed that "[s]imply having a larger assortment of the same thing is not the same as having many different choices" (2001: 2). Vince Carlin added his concern: "While corporate strategies have been cloaked in the language of innovation and consumer choice, the results have so far been the restriction of choice and the postponement of innovation" (2003: 56; also see Mills, 2003, Feb. 13-15; Horwitz, 2005; Edge, 2007).

The question here is that if multiple media platforms (newspapers, television networks and Internet sites) are controlled by the same owner and, *if those platforms share content*, does the fact that there are many different outlets mean that there will be a corresponding number of diverse opinions? The business logic behind convergence would suggest that this would not necessarily be the case.

Media owners are not interested in controlling content

"I buy newspapers to make money to buy more newspapers to make money. As for editorial content, that's the stuff you separate the ads with" (Roy Thomson, as quoted in Clement, 1975: 288). This position, albeit usually stated in less stark terms, has been the argument advanced by Canadian corporate newspaper owners in response to recommendations made to regulate the newspaper industry by both the Davey Senate Committee (Canada, 1970) and the Kent Royal Commission on Newspapers (Canada, 1981) (see Romanow and Soderlund, 1996; Miller, 1998). And while there have been past instances of owner intrusion over issues of content, owners generally placed their interest in turning a profit ahead of their interest in controlling content (see Soderlund and Hildebrandt, 2005). However, the actions of Canwest Global in implementing its "National Editorial/No Contradiction Policy" fundamentally undermined this argument, as with this policy media owners not only demonstrated an interest in content, they demonstrated an interest in controlling that content as well.

In late 2001, Canwest began the National Editorial/No Contradiction Policy for the major daily newspapers it had acquired from Conrad Black's Hollinger Inc. The policy consisted of a series of editorials written on national and international issues by corporate headquarters in Winnipeg and mandated to run in its major newspapers across the country.[4] As a corollary to the policy, individual newspapers were proscribed from writing editorials that contradicted what were referred to as the "core positions" advanced in the national editorials. Initially, two national editorials were projected per week, although this objective was never achieved. Until the practice ceased in the spring of 2003, 36 identified national editorials were published in Canwest newspapers on a variety of topics. Of significance here is that on at least two important questions of public policy—Jean Chrétien's future as the nation's prime minister and appropriate strategies for dealing with the Israel-Palestinian conflict—major Canwest newspapers were restricted from expressing editorial viewpoints that differed from what might be termed the controversial core positions presented by the head office

(Soderlund and Hildebrandt, 2005: 113–119). As well, at the time fears were raised that the policy might create a "chill" in Canwest newsrooms (Moore, 2002). It was argued that journalists would engage in self-censorship so as not to alienate the owners on topics where their views were well known. In short, following the national editorial policy, the question was no longer whether owners would attempt to control content, but rather how far these attempts at controlling content would go.

Attempts to Manage Media Ownership in Canada

Ownership of Canada's media industries has been an issue beginning with the popularization of radio in the 1920s, and Paul Nesbitt-Larking has commented that "the [subsequent] history...is a history of Royal Commissions, and committees, followed by Acts of Parliament... [and that]...bookshelves groan under the weight of state papers" (2001: 58). While it is not our intent here to add unnecessary weight to those bookshelves, we do wish to single out a number of landmark actions in attempts to regulate ownership of the nation's mass media, both broadcast and print.

As P.J. Worsfold has pointed out, "[a]lthough new ideas and perspectives have been introduced, the debate has often returned to the issue of *maintaining diversity* in an increasingly concentrated media landscape" (2007, Mar. 14, italics added). However, the evidence is clear that whatever the recommendations that emerged from a multitude of reports, the results have been greater and greater consolidation of media ownership, culminating in the frenzy of cross-ownership transactions beginning in 2000 that prompted our interest in doing this study.

During the 1920s, whatever regulation of radio broadcasting that existed has been described as "vague and ineffective" (Nesbitt-Larking, 2001: 59). Moreover, radio ownership was dominated by newspapers (private) and the Canadian National Railways (public). The first (and a continuing) challenge to Canadian governments was the need to protect Canada's cultural identity from cross-border intrusions from the United States (see Marlow, 2010, June 9). Arthur Siegel reports that in these early years "Canadian content was less than 20 per cent of programme time. Canada simply plugged into American radio" (1983: 164). The challenge involved more than the importation of American content, as in the absence of regulation; some early Canadian stations in fact operated as direct affiliates of US networks (Romanow and Soderlund, 1996: 123).

In 1929, the Royal Commission on Radio Broadcasting (the Aird Commission) reported to Parliament that "broadcasting can be adequately served only by some form of public ownership operation and control behind which is the national power and prestige of the whole public of the Dominion of Canada" (as quoted in Peers, 1969: 44).

A major initiative on behalf of public ownership was the creation in 1932 of the Canadian Radio Broadcasting Commission (CRBC)—a forerunner of both the Canadian Broadcasting Corporation (CBC) and later the CRTC—as a part of Canada's first Broadcasting Act. Significantly, this act gave the CRBC the power "to lease or to buy any privately owned radio stations." However, a change of government and the Great Depression intervened and the CRBC was frustrated; it had the power but was not given the money to pursue the public ownership option (Romanow and Soderlund, 1996: 128). Thus, from the outset, in spite of a clear preference for public ownership, the Canadian broadcast system emerged as a hybrid of private and public enterprises that has continued to co-exist to this day, sometimes in a less than harmonious fashion.

In 1970, the Canadian government ordered that Canadian broadcasting systems be effectively Canadian-owned. This edict resulted in the forced sale of a number of privately owned broadcast properties, and, as a consequence, created a greater ownership presence for companies such as Power Corporation, Rogers Communications, and Bushnell Communications (Romanow and Soderlund, 1996: 251–252; see also Raboy, 1990). The 1978 *Report of the Royal Commission on Corporate Concentration* (the Bryce Commission) offered a clear direction regarding media ownership concentration—that the ownership of electronic and print media should remain separate. The report recommended that when needed, the CRTC be given the authority "not only to constrain print media from controlling broadcast and electronic media... but also to prevent broadcast media from acquiring or controlling major print media" (Canada, 1978: 353). This policy was to be enforced on a case-by-case basis; by 1994, however, with the approval of the Rogers Communications bid to purchase the holdings of Maclean-Hunter, the policy "fell apart completely" (Romanow and Soderlund, 1996: 256).

Two landmark studies dominate attempts to regulate media ownership in Canada: the Special Senate Committee on Mass Media—the Davey Committee—which examined both print and broadcast media, and the Royal Commission on Newspapers (the Kent Commission).

With respect to concentration of media ownership, the Davey Committee Report pointed out the risks involved in ownership concentration: "What matters is the fact that control of the media is passing into fewer and fewer hands, and that experts agree that the trend is likely to continue and perhaps to accelerate" (Canada, 1970: 6). While the situation was not sufficiently worrisome to merit legislation to undo existing levels of concentration, *enough was enough*. For the Davey Committee, a convincing case had to be made for any further consolidation: "*all* transactions that increase concentration of ownership in the mass media are undesirable and contrary to the public interest— unless shown to be otherwise" (Canada, 1970: 71, italics in the original). The committee's recommendation to create a Press Ownership Review Board to approve or disapprove media consolidations was never acted upon, and a decade later Senator Keith Davey commented "that the situation had gone from 'bad to worse.'...it 'may be in the public interest to have some form of unbundling'" (as quoted in Romanow and Soderlund, 1996: 254).

Thomas Kent, Chairman of the Royal Commission on Newspapers appointed in 1980, agreed. Claiming that there was "too much power in too few hands," the Kent Commission recommended, among other policies, *divestiture* of assets in cases of the most prominent instances of ownership concentration (Canada, 1981: 220). Specific recommendations related to ownership included:

1. The creation of the Canada Newspaper Act, which would be aimed at controlling media concentration, particularly with regard to cross-media and conglomerate ownership.
2. That no further expansion by the Southam group would be sanctioned and that the Thomson group and the Irving family should be required to divest themselves of a selection of their media holdings.
3. That no company should be permitted to own newspapers and television or radio stations in the same market (Worsfold, 2007, Mar. 14).

The recommendations of the Kent Commission (in a somewhat watered-down form) were incorporated into legislation that subsequently died in Parliament.

In the view of Nesbitt-Larking, "the Kent Commission called for only mild regulation of newspaper oligopoly. However, even such moderate measures were rejected by the Liberal and Progressive Conservative administrations of the early 1980s" (2001: 122). Arthur Siegel took a very different position on the Kent Commission report, calling it "one of the most controversial reports ever presented by a Canadian Royal Commission" (1983: 146). With respect to ownership, he took issue with the commission's finding that ownership concentration presented a greater problem in English Canada than in Quebec. For Siegel, "[i]f the principle of extensive concentration is bad, then concentration is as undesirable in the French as in the English press. Further there can be no distinction between 'good' and 'bad' chains, a distinction made by the Commission in its evaluation of the English press" (1983: 149). In a 1999 report on the Davey and Kent reports prepared for the Library of Parliament, Joseph Jackson concludes with the salient point that "the ongoing trend towards concentration and chain ownership means that the link between newspaper ownership and content continues to require clarification" (1999, Dec. 17). It is precisely this *link between ownership and content* that is at the heart of the present study.

The 2001 report of the Commission de la culture to the Quebec National Assembly (QNA), which recommended greater accountability and transparency from media companies, was followed by the creation of a working group led by professor and former journalist Armande Saint-Jean. Its report, submitted in 2003, recommended a series of measures to monitor ownership and requirements for media companies in order to provide "guarantees" of professionalism and independence. This report was not well received by the industry, the Fédération professionnelle des journalistes du Québec and the Press Council, because of potential interference of the state in a supposedly free press. And, reminiscent of the Davey and Kent reports, none of its recommendations were implemented (see Centre d'études sur les médias, n.d.: 6–7).

The *Interim Report* of the Standing Senate Committee on Transport and Communications (Canada, 2004) offered what can only be described as contrasting points of view regarding the effect of convergence on control of content and a possible resulting loss of diversity. Among those citing negative consequences, *Toronto Star* columnist and former *Ottawa Citizen* editor James Travers argued "[t]hat a dominant owner could lead to self-censorship by journalists and a corresponding decrease in the diversity of viewpoints" (Canada, 2004: 65). In her testimony before the committee, Lise Lareau, President of the Canadian Media Guild, addressed the probable effect of "multitasking" journalists, arguing that "there is no question that those are developments that also lead to fewer points of view out there and fewer eyeballs on a story. This is what happens in the markets you are referring to with the cross-ownership issue" (Canada, 2004: 71).

In spite of such concerns, there was a dearth of evidence presented to the committee to support the view that convergence actually had reduced the diversity of content appearing in Canadian media. A number of witnesses appearing before the committee made this point. For example, Professor Armande Saint-Jean of the Université de Sherbrooke, and Chair of the 2003 Quebec task force on news quality and diversity mentioned above, noted that "diversity of ownership does not guarantee diversity of opinion." She went on to point out, however, that "[t]hus far, we are short of any sound evidence or research that would give us a nuanced or detailed portrait of the situation concerning diversity" (Canada, 2004: 59). As well, Neil Seeman of the Fraser Institute claimed that "[t]he scholarship concerning the impact of media convergence and cross-ownership on the quality of news has been sketchy, contradictory and mostly superficial" (Canada, 2004: 70). When Vince Carlin, then Professor of Journalism at Ryerson University, was asked "whether there was any evidence that cross-ownership had produced a commonality of view that reduces the diversity of information generally available to the Canadian public," he replied that to his knowledge, "there is no academic study to prove this, although there is anecdotal evidence" (Canada, 2004: 65). The strongest statement challenging the negative impact of convergence on content diversity came from Phillip Lind, Vice-Chairman of Rogers Communications, who argued that "concerns regarding cross-media ownership rest on the premise that cross-media ownership prevents Canadians from having access to a diverse source of news and information services. We strongly disagree with this premise" (Canada, 2004: 66).

However, journalists and the Canadian public appeared to think otherwise. About 95 per cent of journalists surveyed for the February 2003 McGill University conference, Who Controls Canada's Media, claimed that convergence had a negative impact on newspaper credibility (Soroka and Fournier, 2003, Feb. 11). Results of an Environics poll reported at the same conference indicated that 57 per cent of Canadians saw convergence as a "bad development," as opposed to 36 per cent who saw it in a positive light (Jedwab, 2003, Feb. 10). The latter results were confirmed by a poll dealing with the credibility of Canadian media: according to this study,

56 per cent of Canadians believed that consolidation of media ownership was having a negative impact on their trust in the media (Canadian Media Research Consortium, 2004). A survey of journalists conducted by the National Guild of Canadian Media and the Manufacturing, Professional and Service Workers/Communications Workers of America (TNG Canada) presented to the Senate Committee likewise revealed concerns: 44 per cent of respondents pointed to "a very serious problem...[resulting from]...a loss of local independence in editorial policy in newspapers owned by large chains." On a number of dimensions, strong percentages of respondents claimed that negative consequences were "somewhat or very likely" to stem from media concentration: an overall decline in newspaper quality (71.3 per cent); "programming decisions placed in too few hands" (89.6 per cent); "fewer points of view offered by local media" (83.2 per cent); a reduction in the quality of news coverage (82.4 per cent); and a decrease in "the number of local stories covered by newspapers" (66.4 per cent) (Canada, 2004: 59). A study of journalists working for major media companies in Quebec also found varying levels of job satisfaction related to corporate ownership pressures: job satisfaction was reported highest at Radio-Canada and lowest at Quebecor, with Gesca journalists in between (Bernier, 2008). While, with the exception of Canwest's National Editorial/No Contradiction Policy, hard evidence pointing to negative consequences might be wanting, media ownership convergence certainly appears to lack support among both journalists and Canadians at large.[5]

Conclusion

It would appear that if content-sharing was advanced by media conglomerates as necessary to reduce costs resulting from the fragmentation of both media audiences and platforms, logically we should expect to find content that is "more similar" appearing in media outlets operating under the control of those conglomerates. And while we acknowledge that actual evidence of content-sharing engaged in by these multimedia giants may be scarce, Canwest Global, CTVglobemedia, and Quebecor appeared either to have restructured or were in the process of restructuring to take advantage of content-sharing between their newspaper and television assets.

While recommendations regarding how to deal with the problems created by media ownership concentration vary greatly, it has long been recognized by scholars that dominant societal elites have tremendous potential power to control the access of marginalized groups (and consequently their views) to mass media (see Commission on Freedom of the Press, 1947; Miliband, 1969; Schiller, 1973; Merrill, 1974; Picard, 1985; Herman and Chomsky, 1988; Van Dijk, 1988; Hackett and Zhao, 1998; Taras, 2001). Moreover, in Canwest Global's National Editorial/No Contradiction Policy, we have evidence that this potential power was actually used. Where, as is the case in Canada, divisions based on culture and region are long-standing and those between urban and rural interests are growing (see Henderson, 2004; Wasko and O'Neill, 2007), such divisions cannot in our opinion be best addressed by a "one-voiced media."[6] Since convergence took hold in Canada at the beginning of the new century, not withstanding the recent breakup of Canwest Global and CTVglobemedia, we have seen a considerable narrowing of the elites controlling these access points. However, the consequences for Canadian democracy entailed in this narrowing have yet to be assessed.

Midway through the decade in January 2005, Matthew Fraser, then Editor-in-Chief of the *National Post*, appeared on a panel with fellow Toronto newspaper editors Edward Greenspon (*Globe and Mail*) and Giles Gherson (*Toronto Star*) and reiterated the economic argument underlying strategies of convergence:

> The media environment is disaggregating into these fragments and what larger companies like Canwest Global Communications and Bell Globemedia and Torstar Corp. are doing is to reaggregate those fragments....We will own newspapers and Web sites and own television stations and serve our customers and our readers with those various platforms.
>
> We are not worried whether they are reading the newspaper or just the Web site....It is a reality that the media landscape is disaggregating into fragments and the commercial challenge is to reaggregate those fragments (as quoted in Brent, 2005, Jan. 26: FP2).

The 2005 restructuring of the ownership of Bell Globemedia to include media giant Torstar served to confirm that the convergence of media ownership in Canada was far from dead. Quite to the contrary, as Gordon Pitts has noted, "In an industry with copycat tendencies, that linkage could spark a new round of mergers and acquisitions. It may not be as dramatic as the mega-deals of 2000–2002 that radically redrew the media map. But the search for revenue growth among the industry's power players will intensify" (2005, Dec. 3: B5).[7]

One of the commercial challenges to media profitability is the reality that content is expensive to create in that it requires journalistic talent in news-gathering, writing, editing and presentation that must be compensated. In decades past, wire services such as The Associated Press and The Canadian Press permitted media owners to spread the costs of national and international news-gathering over a wide base of newspapers and television networks. Strategies of corporate convergence that allow for common content to appear in newspapers, the Internet and on television newscasts obviously open new possibilities for spreading the costs of content acquisition over different types of media within one corporate entity.[8]

As Mr. Fraser's comments reaffirmed, "reaggregating fragments" in order to achieve economies of scale continued to form the rationale for Canwest's pursuit of convergence. They also point to the wide acceptance of the idea of convergence in the media industry at large; since he spoke, the strategy of "fragment reaggregation" appears to have taken hold at Quebecor (see chapters 5 and 6, this volume) and perhaps at CTVglobemedia as well, although given the confused ownership/management situation of the latter, that situation was far from clear (see Postscript, this volume).

Benjamin Page has presented a convincing case that a system of mass media that is open to diverse ideas is critical to the successful operation of democratic governance:

> Public deliberation is essential to democracy, in order to ensure that the public's policy preferences—upon which democratic decisions are based—are informed, enlightened, and authentic. In modern societies, however, public deliberation is (and probably must be) largely *mediated*, with professional communicators rather than ordinary citizens talking to each other and to the public through mass media of communication (1996: 1, italics in the original).

In 2001, Canada appeared situated at the beginning point of a significant transformation in the structure of corporate ownership of its mass media that *could* have resulted in a significant reduction in the variety of viewpoints available to the mass public. The incorporation of the *Toronto Star* into the ownership structure of CTVglobemedia in 2005 was potentially significant as well, as it resulted in the last newspaper chain in English-speaking Canada serving major markets linking up with a television network in the form of convergent ownership. From the perspective of democratic theory, this was not a reassuring development.[9]

Moreover, in assessing the impact of the trend toward convergent ownership on diversity of information, it is significant to remember that television and newspapers, while losing ground to the Internet, are still the leading sources of daily news for most Canadians.[10] Further, it is important to bear in mind that prior to 2000, while ownership of both newspapers and television networks was highly concentrated, these two types of media were by and large owned by different sets of companies. Beginning with the dawn of the 21st century, this pattern of ownership changed both quickly and significantly in terms of scale. By the end of 2005, all three major corporate owners of both television and newspaper properties appeared to be following corporate strategies to promote synergies between their print and television holdings, and we felt this development should not escape the attention of those concerned with the health of Canadian democracy.

Organization of the Book

In the pages that follow, chapter 2 reviews research literature on media convergence (most of which focused on the United States), dealing with the meaning of the term and its purported advantages as well as problems encountered in its implementation. This chapter also outlines the research design employed in our empirical study, the results of which are reported in chapters 3 and 4. These chapters present the study's findings at the national level for Canwest, CTVglobemedia and Quebecor, and at the local level for Canwest's television and newspaper properties in Edmonton, Alberta, respectively, along with discussions and interpretations of these findings. Chapters 5 and 6 report the results of our interviews with key media industry stakeholders and discuss not only why convergence-inspired content-sharing did not materialize, but where Canadian media industries are likely headed over the next five years and which strategies they will employ to meet the challenge of "new media." Chapter 7 reviews our conclusions and presents an overall assessment of key issues facing Canadian media during the second decade of the new century and beyond, while the Postscript addresses key developments in media ownership as close to publication as possible.

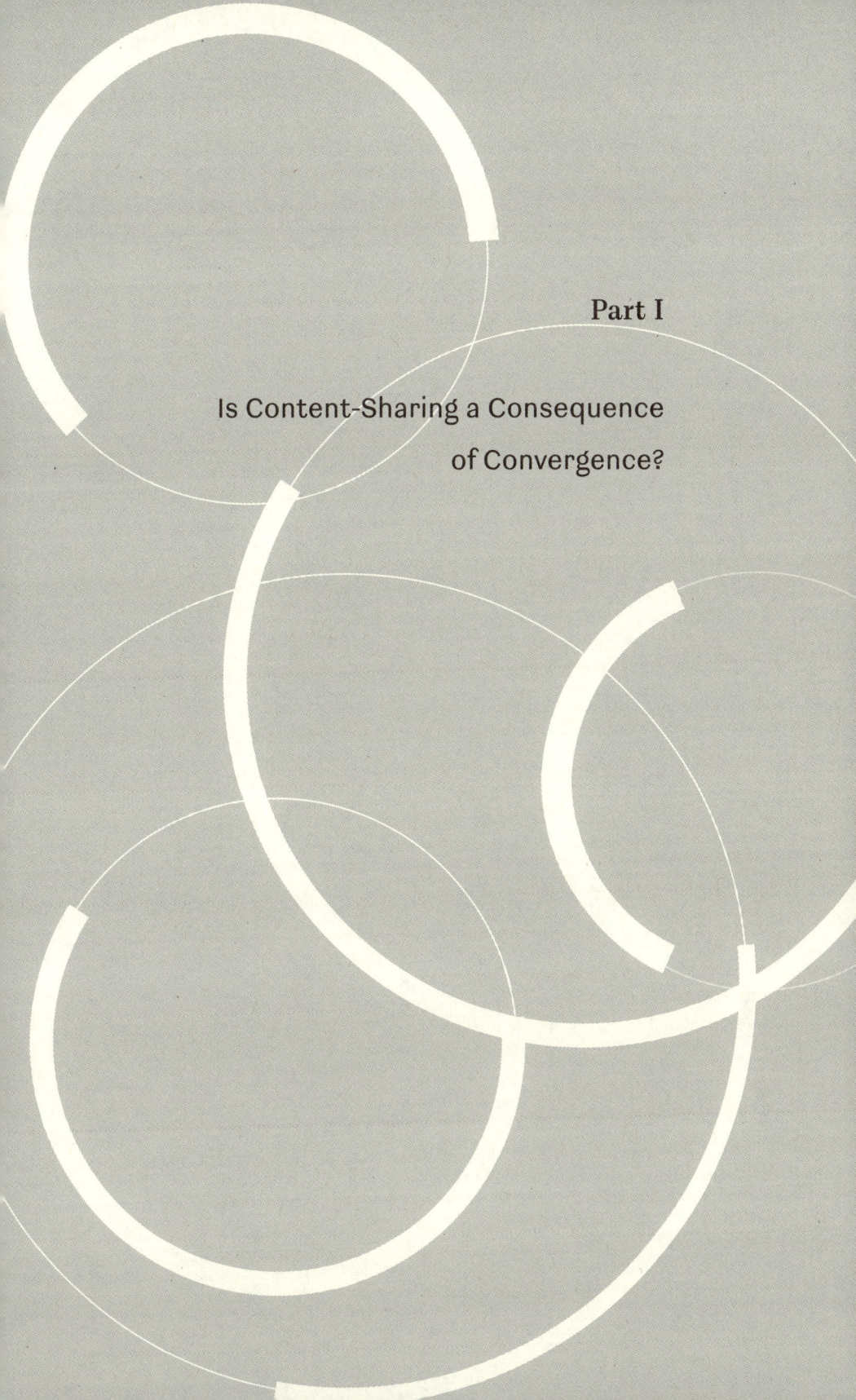

Part I

Is Content-Sharing a Consequence of Convergence?

2

Convergence: Promises and Problems

Background to Convergence

AS OUTLINED IN THE PREVIOUS CHAPTER, for decades critics have been sounding the alarm over the concentration of print media ownership. At the same time, the trend in the newspaper industry has been to consolidate and engage in practices that reduce ownership to fewer and fewer hands. The argument in favour of concentration of ownership is based largely on economies of scale: the bigger the press, the better the ability to disseminate information at a lower cost. While concentration of newspaper ownership is not new, changes in regulatory environments around the world, including Canada, that allow corporations to simultaneously own newspapers and television stations in the same market have resulted in renewed and heightened concern among critics (see Edge, 2007; Winseck, 2008). On March 13, 2003, in response to the changing media environment, the Standing Senate Committee on Transport and Communications initiated a study of the Canadian media industry and its *Final Report*, released on April 27, 2006 (Canada, 2006), examined the impact of concentration of ownership on diversity of information in the Canadian news media. In addition, on September 17, 2007, the CRTC launched a series of public hearings to develop new policies regarding cross-media ownership.

Both the Senate Committee report and new CRTC policies stem from concerns raised by media critics about the potential of cross-owned media not serving the public interest (see chapter 1, this volume). The CRTC's hearings resulted in the January 15, 2008, change in regulatory policy that followed from an examination of three key issues: "the plurality of commercial editorial voices," "the diversity of programming choices offered to Canadians," and "the effectiveness of existing and proposed safeguards with respect to journalistic content in cross-media ownership situations" (CRTC, 2008-4: A4). While the CRTC does not deny that there are many individuals working in various newspapers and television stations across the country, the commission specifically advances a definition of "commercial editorial voices" as "*the number of separately owned voices*" (CRTC, 2008-4: B1, 15, italics added). And, the commission argues, with "separately owned voices" there will be separate editorial and programming resources. This argument is based on the premise that "a diversity of voices is preserved because no one person—no one voice—within an element has sole responsibility for choosing the programming to which Canadians have access" (CRTC, 2008-4: B1, 15). It is clear that the CRTC's concern over media concentration is based on the assumption that the owner of a media company is in fact able to control the editorial content of the various holdings owned by that company. Moreover, the commission signalled that it would "carefully examine transactions that would result in the control by one person of between 35 per cent and 45 per cent of total audience share" for pay, specialty and over-the-air television.

New regulatory requirements with respect to cross-ownership were in fact enacted by the CRTC:

> The Commission, as a general rule, will not approve of a change in the effective control of broadcasting undertakings that would result in the ownership or control, by one person, of a local radio station, a local television station and a local newspaper serving the same market (CRTC, 2008-4: B 64).

[Also],

> Where a person that controls a local radio station and a local television station acquires a local newspaper serving the same market, the Commission will, at the earliest opportunity, require the licensee to

explain why, in light of this policy, its radio or television licence(s) should be renewed (CRTC, 2008-4: B 65).

This view of editorial control is not unique to the CRTC. In its 2006–2007 *Annual Report*, CBC President Robert Rabinovitch claimed that "ownership of Canadian media is becoming concentrated in a few very large companies offering an ever-wider range of services but a declining diversity of opinion and perspectives" (CBC, 2007: 2). Similarly, Marvin Kalb and Amy Sullivan argue that while the proliferation of different types of media is a good thing, they point out "there may be more ways to get 'news,' but the news seems to be all the same" (2000: 4).

A skeptical view of ownership control has its roots in the cultural criticism school of the media. Proponents of this view are many and their writings are extensive (see for example, Picard et al., 1988; Compaine and Gomery, 2000; Winter, 2002, May/June; Bagdikian, 2004; Soderlund and Hildebrandt, 2005; Gingras, 2006; Baker, 2007; George, 2007). The common argument advanced by these scholars is that by having so few owners, the *potential* for editorial abuse is high.

Simone Murray notes that the changes in technology that make "information" or "programming" merely "content" blurs the lines of the different forms of communication. Where at one time the constraints of the medium meant that television programs had to be seen on a television set and that newspapers could only be read in hard copy, those limitations no longer exist. As a result, "the commercial ideal is for commodified content to flow between mediums almost at managerial will, rather than being coterminous with any one specific medium" (Murray, 2003: 10). This, as David Skinner and Mike Gasher note, leads to the potential for abuse, in that converged media can

> aggregate audiences across media and thus increase their market power; reuse programming and editorial content in a number of platforms to increase efficiency; increase their potential ideological clout to decrease diversity and inhibit dissent; and build up significant barriers to entry for new enterprises or competitors (2005: 53).

Using provocative double entendres such as "(Almost) everywhere they are in chains," scholars such as Paul Nesbitt-Larking (2001) invoke an image of the tyranny of a minority of newspaper owners imposing their views on journalists and, in turn, on unsuspecting readers and audiences. While the rhetorical flourish and logic of these arguments is quite compelling, evidence to support the thesis that owners exercise such control is more difficult to find. In research done for the Kent Commission, Fred Fletcher reported that "the negative effects of chain ownership on public affairs coverage, if any, are subtle and difficult to measure. The case against chains rests on a few examples, and some circumstantial evidence, and the obvious potential for abuse" (1981: 46). One such case has been reported in Erin Steuter's study of Irving newspapers' coverage of an Irving Oil refinery strike in New Brunswick (1999). However, as in Fletcher's earlier assessment, the evidence for ownership control is subtle and open to interpretation (Soderlund and Hildebrandt, 2005: 42–43).

In the US context, Daniel Chomsky offers quite damning evidence in the form of memos written from 1947 to 1961 by *New York Times* publisher Arthur Hays Sulzberger to his editor Turner Cateledge to show the power the publisher had in influencing news content. Chomsky points out that there are "gaps in the documentary record," which suggests to him that "the true frequency of ownership intervention was higher" (2006: 15). Moreover, he argues that the measure of ownership influence he used "probably underestimates the true influence of ownership," contending that "[t]he internal record reveals processes and practices that systematically conceal the owner's power. The owner can establish broad policies...that are designed not only to shape a single story but to shape uncountable stories" (2006: 15).

Despite the evidence provided by Chomsky in the case of the *New York Times*, there are in fact few current documented examples of owners of converged companies exercising such editorial control. No doubt many would argue, as does Chomsky, that this does not prove that owners do not exercise editorial control, it is just that publishers and editors may not keep records, or that those records are not publicly available. This limitation aside, the most cited example of overt owner control over content in a converged media company is that of Canwest's decision to run national editorials (see chapter 1, this volume; also see Khan, 2002; Moore, 2002; Luzadder, 2003; Shade, 2005; Soderlund and Hildebrandt, 2005; Balingall, 2006; Knox, 2008). Leslie Shade cites the national editorial policy as "an exemplar of many of the structural problems inherent in media concentration in an era of media convergence, such as diminution of journalistic freedom and integrity, shrinking of local content, and the decline of public interest values" (2005: 101), while

Paul Knox points out that "rarely, if ever, have so many disciplinary measures been imposed and chain-wide warnings issued concurrently by a media proprietor in Canada on an issue of journalistic principles" (2008: 516). Others, writing at the time, claimed that this would be just the beginning as the company and its policies would inevitably expand into the United States (Moore, 2002: 11; Luzadder, 2003: 7), and Ben Scott expressed concern that Canwest and other conglomerates would dilute the "diversity of views in their communities" (2005: 116).

Nonetheless, in part as a result of the public outcry, as well as the vocal opposition of journalists, Canwest stopped imposing its national editorials. This, however, did not silence critics "who warned that the Asper family bias would remain in place" (Edge, 2005: 12). While Canwest pulled back from its national editorial policy, until encountering bankruptcy in 2009, its status as a powerful entity in the Canadian media landscape remained undiminished as it owned radio, television and digital specialty services, as well as the major dailies, and more recently, weekly newspapers across the country (CRTC, 2008-02-11).

Convergence: The Concept and Its Track Record

A major problem with the term *convergence* is that there is no one agreed upon definition. As Stephen Quinn observes, "convergence probably has as many definitions as the number of people who attempt to define it" (2004: 111). He adds that for some, "convergence involves a reporter who is a specialist in a particular area being able to re-purpose information so that the reporters' expertise appears in several forms" (2004: 112). In some US markets, as in Canada, the same company owns both the local television station and the local daily paper.[1] The theory behind such combinations holds that the television outlet will benefit from the larger staff of the newspaper and be able to provide more depth to the story than would the resources of the television newsroom alone. Apart from sharing staff, another economic benefit pointed to is the cross-promotion of stories (Quinn, 2004: 112).

Elizabeth Birge has called convergence a "squishy term" (as quoted in Sands, 2004, May 17), while Gordon Pitts has described it as a "vague concept" (2002: 4)—and these characterizations are not without justification (also see Gordon, 2003; Sauvageau, 2003; Lavoie, 2004). Other researchers have attempted to add specificity to definitions of convergence. Rich Gordon (2003), for example, states that convergence can relate to ownership, tactics, structure, and information, or storytelling. For his part, David Taras argues that there are four realms of convergence: "the convergence of technologies, the convergence of corporations, the convergence of information with entertainment and the convergence of cultures" (2001: 61), while José Alberto García Avilés and colleagues describe it as dynamic and multidimensional, involving "technological, managerial, communicative and professional [perspectives], all of which are intertwined in a continuously changing media environment" (2009: 286). Thorsten Quandt and Jane Singer have referred to convergence as "the blending or merging of formerly distinct media technologies, mainly based on digitization processes." They offer further that "[j]ournalism researchers have primarily focused on 'newsroom convergence,' particularly in relation to changes in work routines and organizational structures connected to the production of content across media platforms" (2009: 130). The present study of the impact of ownership convergence on Canadian media content follows this definition, as we undertake a comparison of content in pairs of television and newspaper news stories from both cross-owned and separately owned television-newspaper ownership structures.

As pointed out in chapter 1, in terms of protecting democracy, it can be argued that the most important type of convergence relates to its impact on the content conveyed by mass media. While critics worry that informational convergence will lead to fewer voices and less diversity in news, corporate owners see it as the future of information dissemination at a reasonable cost. Specifically, corporate managers see informational convergence as a cost-saving measure that can be realized; for example, when one journalist writes a story for the corporation's newspaper print edition, provides additional information for the online platform, and serves as an expert source in an interview with the corporation's television news or public affairs program. As Quinn points out, "The technology exists where information can be gathered by one person and repackaged into different media for presentation" (2004: 114). This was certainly the vision that Canwest President and CEO Leonard Asper had in mind when in a 2001 speech he mused that

> [i]n the future, journalists will wake up, write a story for the web, write a column, take their cameras, cover an event and do a report for TV and file a video clip for the web. What we have really acquired is a

quantum leap in the product we offer advertisers and a massive, creative, content generation machine.

These multitasking journalists are disparagingly described in the literature as "Inspector Gadgets" or "platypus journalists," since they must do all tasks, but not necessarily do any of them well (Quinn, 2004: 113). Nonetheless, media managers, and not just those in the private sector, see multitasking as an attractive possibility. For example, in November 2007 the public broadcaster CBC began a restructuring plan that involved consolidating news-gathering to "deliver news more efficiently across its radio, television and online divisions" (*Windsor Star*, 2008, Feb. 21: B1). By February 2008, CBC announced that it would merge its radio and television production operations and continue to integrate its various news operations (Dixon, 2008, Feb. 21).

While Mr. Asper and others acknowledge that the technology exists for this type of journalism, most agree that it would involve an extensive restructuring based upon how the corporation envisions convergence working. According to Ben Scott, "Convergence in journalism does not refer primarily to the technological reduction of all communication to a digital form. It refers to a new strategy in the economic management of information production and distribution" (2005: 101). As a consequence, there are many ways in which news organizations can converge. The approach described by Mr. Asper above is what Scott calls "a cross between newsroom convergence and cross-media partnerships," in that a corporation has a common software that

> swiftly aggregates, collates, and distributes digitized text, audio, and video between the nodes on the corporate network. The virtues of this common production platform allow for cross-media content sharing, the elimination of duplicate reporting, and cross-promotional opportunities (2005: 103).

It is significant that Scott cited Canwest Interactive as having one of the best integrated uses of this technology in its website Canada.com.

The rationale for convergence is that it lends itself to digital information dissemination on diverse platforms such as the Internet, podcasts and personal digital assistants (hand-held devices). However, there is less certainty of how convergence will work in the "old media" consisting of newspapers and television. While there is much debate over how much the Internet will bleed advertising away from newspapers, the larger concern is that the relaxation of regulations allows organizations such as Canwest to consolidate operations in markets where it owns both newspapers and television stations. This holds as well for concerns over the merger that led to CTVglobemedia, where the largest national private broadcaster (CTV) is owned by the same corporation as the national newspaper of record (*Globe and Mail*), and for Quebecor, which owns TVA, the most popular French-language television network, and major daily newspapers in Montreal and Quebec City, accounting for half the total circulation in Quebec, as well as the English-language newspapers of the Sun Media chain. What needs to be assessed is to what extent the dream espoused by Leonard Asper, or the nightmare feared by the critics, has come to fruition.

Larry Dailey and his colleagues have outlined a continuum of types of convergence that helps us understand the degree of convergence that a news organization may adopt. For the authors, this continuum acknowledges that there are "overlapping levels of cross-promotion, cloning, coopetition, content sharing, and full convergence" (Dailey et al., 2005a: 151). In other words, while a media empire may well have developed some elements of cross-promotion, this can be quite different from full convergence. Dailey and his associates provide the following definitions for the components of a convergence continuum:

> *Cross-promotion* is the process of using words and/or visual elements to promote content by the partner and appearing in the partner's medium (e.g., when a newscaster urges the viewers to read a story appearing in the newspaper or the newspaper publishes the logo of the television partner).
>
> *Cloning* is essentially unedited display of a partner's product (e.g., content from a newspaper or newscast that is republished on the partner's Web site or jointly operated Web portal).
>
> *Coopetition* is the point at which partners cooperate by sharing information on selected stories, but still compete and produce original content (e.g., when a newspaper reporter appears on a newscast as an expert to discuss a story or a broadcaster allows a print photographer to ride on the station helicopter to cover breaking news).

Content sharing exists when the partners meet regularly to exchange ideas and jointly develop special projects (e.g., election coverage or investigative work).

Convergence is the level at which partners have a shared assignment/editor's desk and the story is developed by team members who use the strengths of each medium to best tell the story (e.g., a multimedia project that contains in-depth text for print and Web, still photos and video, audio, graphics, searchable databases and other interactive elements) (Dailey et al., 2005a: 153).

The rationale for the continuum approach is the acknowledgement that media production is fluid and that despite cost savings associated with convergence, there are some basic problems to be confronted in making it work on a day-to-day basis. The most daunting of these are the resources that need to be harnessed to allow for full convergence to take place. For starters, at the practical level, for there to be full convergence, journalists working in different media need to be physically closer. This means sharing newsrooms, editorial meetings and sources. This requires massive staff reorganization, as well as money, time and energy (Filak, 2004: 217). When we began our study in 2006, there were in fact only a few American newsrooms that had undergone this type of transformation (Duhe et al., 2004).

The most studied of these is the convergence of newsrooms in Tampa, Florida, where television station WFLA-TV, local news site TBO.com and the *Tampa Tribune* were merged to create the News Center (Wendland, 2001, Feb. 21). Not only did the three media platforms share resources and space, they routinely held common editorial meetings. This led some researchers to hypothesize that full convergence of these newsrooms would be achieved. It was felt that as journalists formed social bonds, the traditional barriers between print and electronic media would break down. To date, however, these expectations have not been fulfilled. Research has found that while journalists shared "tips and information across the media platforms," they did not engage in the other elements of convergence (Huang et al., 2004: 86). Another study of media convergence at two companies in Oklahoma City found "little convergence between the partners." Moreover, the little that had been achieved was deemed to be "poorly coordinated" (Ketterer et al., 2004: 61). This outcome was consistent with surveys of journalists that found that after initial experiments with convergence, as time went on, journalists went back to working on their own (Kraepling and Criado, 2006: 60). Other studies found that it just was not cost-effective to engage in this type of convergence (Singer, 2004a: 16; for studies of convergence practices in Europe, see Avilés and Carvajal, 2008 and Avilés et al., 2009; Gestin et al., 2009).

As for the concern of critics that conglomerate news would provide fewer stories and less diversity, empirical studies have also failed to confirm those fears. Instead, some research has found evidence supporting the argument of media owners that convergence allows for better and more coverage. For example, in a point-in-time comparison, Brian Schaffner and Michael Wagner report that

> [s]tations owned by larger companies actually produce *more* coverage of these [US Senate] campaigns and are *more* likely to air debates during the campaign. In addition, cross-owned stations (those owned by a company owning a newspaper in the same market) also produce substantially more coverage than other stations (2006: 1, italics in the original).

With respect to the charge that convergence produces less diversity of editorial content, in a study comparing cross-owned TV and newspaper content, David Pritchard found that the slant of coverage on television was different from newspaper coverage; as well, it "often contradicted the newspaper's endorsement of a candidate" (2002: 10). A five-year study of local news by Tom Rosenstiel and Amy Mitchell found that ownership did make a difference, but evidence regarding the impact of cross-ownership was mixed. Smaller station groups produced higher quality newscasts than larger station groups. At the same time, network-affiliated stations also produced higher quality newscasts than network-owned and operated stations. However, stations characterized by cross-ownership had higher quality newscasts than those that were not cross-owned. Rosenstiel and Mitchell also found that "local ownership offered little protection against newscasts being very poor, and did not produce superior quality" (2003: 1).

The idea that there is a hierarchy of influences determining media content is advanced by Pamela Shoemaker and Stephen Reese. According to their research, "professional roles and ethics have a direct effect on mass media content, whereas the effect of personal attitudes, values and beliefs on mass media content is indirect" (1996: 55). In fact, much of the research done in the United States has found that lack of content convergence is not due to the fact that owners are reluctant to implement it, but rather because journalists, either overtly or inadvertently, place obstacles in the way of such changes. Some contend that newsrooms have their own "cultures," defined as a "set of shared attitudes, values, goals and practices" (Singer, 2004b: 846). Put succinctly, newspaper journalists have professional values in areas such as "expertise, ethics, public service, and autonomy, plus work routines" that differ from those of television or radio reporters (Singer, 2004b: 846). As a consequence, journalists themselves resist convergence, or sharing news, as a matter of professional disdain for their counterparts in other media (see Gormley, 1976; Lawson-Borders, 2006). American research has found that despite management's desire for full convergence, reporters on the ground are reluctant to make this part of their daily work habits. Some of this reluctance is a consequence of journalists feeling territorial over stories and not wanting to lose a story to a different medium, regardless of whether it is owned by the same company (Filak, 2004: 217). More recent studies point to less journalistic resistance. For example, Quandt and Singer refer to a "potentially significant shift in newsroom culture," including a more open style of management, and "open communication channels" between journalists working in converged newsrooms. The major issues of contention are now workload and compensation (2009: 135–136).

As William Silcock and Susan Keith found in their survey of journalists, "[h]aving a TV journalist write for one of the newspapers usually was, with a few exceptions, considered a waste of resources" (2006: 617). In part this was due to the view that the different types of journalists sometimes had conflicting goals. For example, there was a perception that videography's only aim was "to make you look good," in contrast to newspaper photography, which has a cultural norm to "capture life as it is" (2006: 619). As a result of these cultural biases, a Phoenix-based convergence partner decided to abandon plans to have newspaper photographers shoot video (Silcock and Keith, 2006: 619). Moreover, each medium has its own culture in terms of language used and the methods of gathering news (Lawson-Borders, 2006: 16). Thus, convergence is not a static element; rather it has been shown to evolve, and sometimes devolve, as a result of different influences. Wilson Lowrey found, for example, "that the more time that news organizations spend partnering, the less favorable are managers' attitudes" (2006: 254).

Another concern is that the traditional media have their particular "skill sets" that do not translate well when carrying out convergence. The argument is made that because newspapers tend to provide more in-depth coverage, print journalists will be reluctant to file stories on television. Similarly, television journalists may not have the depth of knowledge on an issue to provide content for newspapers. As a result, it is argued, the most that will happen is that news organizations will share content, but each type of journalist will specialize in his or her own medium (Huang et al., 2004: 77; see also chapter 7, note 3, this volume).

To date there really has not been a concerted empirical effort to map out the extent to which media content in Canada has been affected by ownership convergence. If we apply the convergence continuum developed by Dailey et al. to Canada, we are certainly able to cite many examples of routine cross-promotion. But that is not necessarily a new phenomenon. Since at least 1999, CTV *News* and the *Globe and Mail* have cooperated on public opinion polls, not only cross-promoting each other's news, but sharing information as well as reporters. This, of course, predates the merger of their ownership structure in 2000. The question post-2000 is whether CTV and the *Globe and Mail* have gone beyond the sharing of poll data to sharing other aspects of news production. In Quebec, there was as well a partnership agreement between Gesca-owned *La Presse* and Radio-Canada in response to Quebecor's purchase of TVA in 2000.

We can also see that in the content of "all-news channels" there is a good deal of cross-promotion and coopetition. Both CTV and CBC news cable channels have daily shows that focus on Canadian politics and interviews with Canadian politicians. A few years ago, programs such as CTV Newsnet's *Mike Duffy* and CBC's *Politics* hosted by Don Newman regularly interviewed journalists from other news organizations. The main journalists featured on Mike Duffy's program were Craig Oliver (*CTV News*) and Jane Taber (*Globe and Mail*) who were also co-hosts of another CTV program, *Question Period*. However, in addition to these journalists who were regularly interviewed on the program, Duffy also hosted journalist panels consisting of reporters from the *Toronto Star* as well as Canwest publications.[2]

A search of the Virtual News Library of the transcripts of CTV's *Mike Duffy* program (May 20, 2005 to February 12, 2008) found that 534 journalists had appeared on the program. Overall, *Globe and Mail* journalists appeared most often at 30.3 per cent, with CTV journalists following close behind at 27 per cent. This is consistent with the theory that convergence involves cross-promotion and coopetition. By interviewing opinion writers from the *Globe and Mail*, the *Mike Duffy* show encouraged viewers to pick up the next day's paper. This was not full coopetition, however, as *Globe* journalists were not doing exclusive reports for CTV, but rather expressing their opinions on the political events of the day as part of a panel with other journalists, sometimes from competing news organizations. Similarly, the CTV journalists who appeared helped to promote other CTV programs such as *CTV News*, for which the reporters all filed stories, as well as promoting the Sunday news program, *Question Period*. That program illustrates how CTVglobemedia had moved in this case beyond simple cross-promotion toward full convergence as the hosts were CTV reporter Craig Oliver, and the *Globe and Mail*'s Jane Taber. Both hosts appeared on the Mike Duffy program and their regular affiliation as well as *Question Period* was promoted.

What is somewhat inconsistent with expectations generated in the literature is the fact that in addition to interviewing CTV and *Globe and Mail* reporters, the *Mike Duffy* program also interviewed the *Globe and Mail*'s competitors. For example, Sun Media journalists appeared 11.8 per cent of the time, while *Toronto Star* reporters appeared 6.2 per cent of the time. *La Presse* journalists also received considerable attention, accounting for 10 per cent of guests. In addition, journalists from Canwest, *Maclean's* and other news organizations also appeared on the program. Yet, while the program did not shy away from featuring newspapers competing with the *Globe and Mail*, it did not interview any reporters from competing television networks or stations. Thus, no Canwest television reporters appeared, nor did any CBC television or radio journalists. And, in total, non-CTVglobemedia journalists accounted for 42 per cent of all journalists, compared to CTVglobemedia journalists with 58 per cent of appearances.

Of course, this is just one program and it is difficult to compare these results with those of other public affairs programs. While the closest equivalent to the *Mike Duffy* program was CBC's *Politics*, hosted by Don Newman, the CBC program did not provide publicly accessible transcripts. However, a review of 113 media websites in 2001 and 2003 found that CBC was the most converged news outlet and that the "main advantage resulting from cross-ownership of television and newspapers was the ability to 'cross-promote' media platforms across platforms" (Sparks et al., 2006: 418). There was, however, a similar analysis done in 2008 by the labour group Syndicat des communications de Radio-Canada (SCRC). One-third of on-air analyses (TV and radio) were done by journalists from *La Presse* and other Gesca newspapers. The union denounced this practice of using external collaborators, suggesting that in-house SRC journalists could do the same work (Lemay, 2008). On the other hand, TVA tends to use journalists working at Quebecor newspapers as analysts (Bousquet, 2002). Christopher Hall, a columnist for *Journal de Montréal*, is a regular contributor to Radio-Canada's radio programming and ironically, Sophie Durocher, who wrote a column for Quebecor's free daily *24 heures* criticizing the strong presence of Gesca analysts on Radio-Canada, has been a frequent guest as well (Jodoin, 2010; Durocher, 2010, May 5). Participation in Radio-Canada news and current affairs programs appears to be frowned upon for those working at TVA, although there have been some collaborations on radio programs. Some of these were criticized internally as "taking sides" during the labour contract conflict at *Journal de Québec* (April 2007–August 2008). Journalists from *Journal de Montréal* do not appear to have worked as Radio-Canada analysts since the lockout at that paper in January 2009.

In 2000, the CRTC cleared the way for ownership convergence of television networks with local newspapers (Arab, 2001, July 2). News organizations quickly responded, with Canwest Global Communications owning both local television stations and newspapers, often in the same market. CTV and the *Globe and Mail* also merged, forming Bell Globemedia (now CTVglobemedia) incorporating a national network, cable news channels, including CTV's Newsnet, and the national daily newspaper, the *Globe and Mail*. While newspaper-based Quebecor was allowed to acquire a major television asset, it volunteered to maintain separate newsrooms for its newspaper and television properties, a condition accepted by the CRTC. In that their mergers involved television-based companies buying newspaper chains, these conditions were not applied to Canwest and Bell Globemedia.[3]

Most commentators acknowledge that full convergence takes time to accomplish, as journalistic cultures need to adapt and perhaps new journalists need to be trained to work across a variety of media. Nonetheless, the ownership convergence that has occurred in Canada provides an excellent opportunity to assess empirically the extent to which the significant cross-ownership that has taken place has affected media content. Critics would suggest that we are moving toward full convergence and that Canadian democracy will suffer under the negative effects of fewer reporters and sources, less critical attention, more trivial coverage, as well as less diversity of viewpoints. In contrast, the proponents of convergence, typically news organization owners, argue that there will be more news and better coverage as journalists can specialize and provide more in-depth coverage across media platforms. In this vein, Jean-Pierre Blais, CRTC Executive Director of Broadcasting, pointed out that if media companies "can free up resources through synergies it may actually mean better news coverage on other news stories, because they may be able to spend more money on other stories" (CBC, 2001, Aug. 2). More recently, Quandt and Singer see convergence as far from dead, pointing to the need to

> integrate new formats and new voices to a far greater extent than is currently the case. Journalists in today's converged newsrooms are only beginning to realize the opportunities of this multimedia environment, let alone to harness the capabilities inherent in the various technologies now available to them....The real power of convergence is in relinquishing the power of controlling information and fostering the power of sharing it (2009: 141).

The Study

Pamela Shoemaker and Stephen Reese have pointed out that "[m]edia content is the basis of media impact" (1991: 23), reaffirming Robert Fowler's earlier assessment that "[t]he only thing that really matters in broadcasting is program content; all the rest is housekeeping" (Canada, 1965: 3). Beginning in 2007, we undertook a study that sought to document whether, and to what extent, diversity in media content was actually reduced by concentrated media ownership. Specifically, we sought to find out whether combining television and newspaper platforms under one corporate owner led to news content-sharing among the different outlets controlled by that owner, thereby reducing the range of distinct voices and opinions seen, heard and read in Canada's mainstream mass media. It is important to point out that our study focused on the impact of ownership-inspired content-sharing on Canadian democratic practice—we did not examine content-sharing in the genre of "entertainment." While we do not dispute that entertainment content is a major component of media convergence, it raises issues not directly related to our focus on news and democratic practice. We recognized that various arts play a significant role in creating community identity and that the industrialization of culture, in which mass media play an important role, has democratic implications, but we considered these to fall outside the scope of the present study.

If content-sharing is advanced by a media conglomerate as necessary to reduce its costs resulting from audience fragmentation, we should then expect to find content that is more similar appearing in the media outlets under its control. If the critical question is "how much content-sharing is too much" (Lowry et al., 2004, Feb. 23; see also Mongeau and Amesse, 2001), we need to know first the extent to which content is actually shared in companies pursuing convergence strategies that involve print and broadcast properties.

Research Design

Our research question was addressed through the method of comparative content analysis. For four randomly selected sample weeks in 2007, the research reported in chapter 3 examines the diversity in news content that appeared in flagship newspapers and TV newscasts controlled by Canwest Global, CTVglobemedia and Quebecor, in comparison to control groups composed of non-cross-owned media properties. In turn, chapter 4 addresses whether content-sharing occurs more frequently at the local level than the national level by linking Canwest newspaper and television news content in one local market—that of Edmonton, Alberta.

Each national network newscast was paired with the national daily newspaper controlled by the same owner as shown in Table 2.1. CTV News was paired with the *Globe and Mail*, both owned by CTVglobemedia. *Global National* was paired with the *National Post*, both owned by Canwest Global. For the English-language study, the control group was CBC's *The National*, paired with the independently owned *Winnipeg Free Press* and the Halifax *Chronicle-Herald*. On the French-language side the TVA network's newscast TVA *réseau* was paired with *Le Journal de Montréal*, both owned by Quebecor, while the control group was composed of SRC's *Le Téléjournal* with *La Presse* and *Le Devoir*. For the Edmonton-based comparison, Edmonton Global's *The News Hour* was paired with the *Edmonton Journal*, both Canwest properties. The local

TABLE 2.1   National Media Studied

ctvglobemedia	Canwest Global	Quebecor
TV: *CTV News*	TV: *Global National*	TV: *TVA réseau*
Print: *Globe and Mail*	Print: *National Post*	Print: *Journal de Montréal*
Control Group (English)	**Control Group (French)**	
TV: *The National* (CBC)	TV: *Le Téléjournal* (SRC)	
Print: *Winnipeg Free Press, Chronicle-Herald*	Print: *La Presse, Le Devoir*	

data are also compared to Canwest's national findings as well as those from the national control group.

Sample

During the four sample weeks, we recorded the flagship evening/nightly TV news programs "off air." Stories in each entire news program (minus promos, stock market reports, advertisements and routine weather reports) were identified by topic. These story lists, aggregated for the entire week, formed the base upon which the comparison with corresponding newspaper content appearing during the same week was made.[4] From the full 12-month period of 2007 we randomly selected four weeks, one in each quarter: February 12–17; May 21–26; September 10–15; and December 3–8. This resulted in a 20-day sample for television news programs (five days per week) and a 24-day sample for major daily newspapers (six days per week) (see Rosenstiel and Mitchell, 2003 for the logic of such sampling).

"Paired Comparisons"[5]

Following the taping, news stories were identified by subject; using these TV story lists, the print editions of newspapers were examined to find matching stories to create "story pairs" that were then coded to determine the extent of content similarity. Story pairs did not have to appear on the same or successive days but at any time during the sample week. Once the TV/newspaper story pairs had been selected, trained coders at the University of Windsor and Université Laval were instructed to document descriptive information about each story, such as the date, the position in the newscast or page in the newspaper, the reporters' names and story length, as well as to judge story similarity on five elements to be described below.

Measures of Similarity

It is important to keep in mind that "news" is event-driven (Wolfsfeld, 2004). There is, therefore, an inherent expectation that news stories reporting on the same event will be *similar*, at least to some extent (Sauvageau, 2003). What we needed to determine then was whether some form of content-sharing or other convergence practice might be taking place and hence our task was to develop measures of similarity between items of content that were by their very nature quite likely to be similar.

The first indicator of content-sharing was whether the *same reporter* filed both the paired newspaper and television stories. Beyond this, we used five key indicators to assess the extent of content similarity between stories. On a three-point scale, coders judged the degree of similarity between the television and the newspaper story on each of five elements of news reports.

1. *Story lead*—the extent to which the introductions/leads in the TV and newspaper stories were similar.
2. *Dimensions*—the extent to which the stories covered the same distinct topics. We also counted the number of dimensions in television and newspaper stories.
3. *Language*—the extent to which the same sentence structure, key words or quotes were used in stories.
4. *Sources*—the extent to which the same sources were used in the stories. In addition, the number of sources used in television and newspaper stories was documented.
5. *Editorial "Spin"*—the extent to which the approach to the stories or "evaluations" contained in the coverage was similar.

The operational definitions for the measurement for all five indicators were as follows:

1: *rather different*—the treatments in both media appear independent;
2: *somewhat similar*—there is some resemblance, possibly due to coincidence, the nature of the event, or possibly minimal sharing;
3: *very similar*—the two stories appeared to use the same information to a noticeable degree.

If coders assigned a code of 3, indicating that the pair was "very similar," we asked them to document the evidence leading to that choice and we further investigated that pair of stories. A code of "non-applicable" was assigned if there was not enough information to assign a similarity code on a particular indicator, as in the case of the absence of "spin" or where no sources were identified in the story.

Further, by combining the five indicators, we were able to assess on an aggregate basis the extent to which there might be sharing of reporters, sources or editorial spin. Because all the indicators were measured on the same scale, we were able to calculate the average across all story indicators, allowing us to compare content-sharing practices between three sets of converged media properties as well as control groups of media properties not linked by common ownership.

Intercoder reliability tests were conducted; using Holsti's method (1969: 140), a minimum intercoder reliability coefficient of 82.5 per cent was established and maintained. Following the original coding, each story was reviewed by the authors as to whether it contained elements of cross-promotion, such as encouraging television viewers or newspaper readers to find more information on the story on the outlet's website or from that of the partner news organization.

Hypotheses

H_1: In order to realize advantages of convergence, television and newspaper content in cross-owned media properties will evidence the highest levels and greatest extent of similarity. Conversely, as there are no ownership links between them, television and newspaper content of media properties in the control groups will evidence the least amount of similarity.

H_2: Within the test groups, due to an early commitment to implement convergence strategies, Canwest media will show the highest level and greatest extent of content similarity. Contrariwise, Quebecor-owned media, because of its commitment to the CRTC not to merge editorial functions, will show the least amounts of content similarity, while CTVglobemedia will evidence an intermediate level and extent of similarity.

H_3: Due to the relative ease of implementation of convergence at the local level, the greatest level and extent of content similarity will be found between Canwest's Edmonton properties.

Conclusion

The empirical studies that follow in chapters 3 and 4 examine to what extent, and in what way, convergence has been taking place in Canadian newspapers and television news. The study thus seeks to assess the degree to which convergence was being practiced in 2007 in both English- and French-language Canadian media. If media critics are correct, we should find support for the hypothesis that private cross-owned media engaged more frequently in content-sharing, resulting in higher scores on the various indicators of content similarity than is the case for the control groups consisting of non-ownership-linked media. However, if the results reported from US research hold for Canada, then we should find no statistically significant differences in content similarity between convergent media and non-convergent media, providing support for the null hypothesis that cross-owned media did not share content across their television and newspaper properties.

3

Content-Sharing in National Media

Introduction

IN 2008, THE YEAR FOLLOWING our content analysis, Rogers Communications and Shaw Communications were primarily involved in the content distribution sector (the so-called media pipes), while Quebecor and BCE appeared most advanced in terms of integrating all types of media (print, broadcast, production, distribution and Internet). Only Canwest Global, CTVglobemedia (with the inclusion of Torstar in the ownership structure) and Quebecor, however, had a significant presence in the critical "content assets"—major daily newspapers, prominent Internet sites and conventional television broadcasting networks. Table 3.1 presents an overview of the extent of cross-media ownership in Canada as it existed in 2008.

It should be noted that at the time of our study there were no converged newsrooms in Canada, and that Quebecor specifically had voluntarily offered to the CRTC to refrain from instituting any such merger. This, as well as research in the United States showing limited convergence effects, should not lead us to expect high levels of content-sharing. For example, Dailey et al. found that even in cases of cross-owned television and newspaper properties, most partners did not take advantage of cross-promotion opportunities (2005b: 43). Indeed, this proved to be the case in our study. Throughout the four-week

TABLE 3.1   Cross-Media Ownership in Canada, as of 2008

	Ownership Group	Astral	BCE	Brunswick	Canwest	Cogeco	Corus*	CTVglobemedia	Power Corp.	Quebecor	RNC Media	Rogers	Shaw*	Torstar	Transcontinental
PRINT	Dailies		+	+				+	+	+				+	+
	Weeklies		+	+					+	+				+	+
	Magazines								+	+		+		+	+
BROADCAST	TV: Conventional			+	+	+	+		+	+	+	+	+		
	TV: Pay & Specialty	+		+			+	+	+	+	+	+	+		
	TV			+	+	+	+	+		+		+		+	
	Radio	+		+	+	+	+		+	+	+				
DISTRIBUTION	Cable					+				+		+	+		
	Satellite		+			+	+	+					+		
	Other		+			+	+		+	+					
WEB	Internet portals and sites	+	+	+	+	+	+	+	+	+	+	+		+	+

*Corus and Shaw are distinct properties, but both have the Shaw family as majority shareholders.
Sources: Canada, 2004, updated by the authors with data from Centre d'études sur les médias and the CRTC.

sample of matched story pairs, no television reporter filed a story for a newspaper, and no newspaper reporter filed a story or appeared on a television broadcast regarding the same story.[1] This indicates a clear absence of "coopetition" (Dailey et al., 2005a). Moreover, in terms of overall story content, we found little evidence to support the hypothesis that greater sharing of content would be seen in story pairs from cross-owned media properties. As the following analysis will show, from story leads to language, from sources used to editorial spin of articles, there was a relatively low level of content similarity between television and newspaper stories in both our test and control group pairs.

Findings

For the English-language media, 233 TV/print story pairs were formed for the (cross-owned) test groups, and 219 pairs for the (independently

TABLE 3.2A Story Lead Similarity, by Test and Control Groups (English)

	TEST		CONTROL		TOTAL	
	N	%	N	%	N	%
Rather different	105	45.1	107	48.9	212	46.9
Somewhat similar	101	43.3	84	38.4	185	40.9
Very similar	27	11.6	28	12.8	55	12.2
Total	233	100.0	219	100.1	452	100.0

x^2 = 1.167 df = 2 n.s.

TABLE 3.2B Story Lead Similarity, by Test and Control Groups (French)

	TEST		CONTRÔLE		TOTAL	
	N	%	N	%	N	%
Plutôt différent	18	9.9	35	10.0	53	10.0
Assez semblable	109	60.2	244	69.9	353	66.6
Très semblable	54	29.8	70	20.1	124	23.4
Total	181	99.9	349	100.0	530	100.0

x^2 = 6.552 df = 2 Sig. = .038 Phi = .111 Cramer's V = .111

owned) control groups, for a total of 452 units. The French-language sample yielded 181 pairs in the test group and 349 pairs in the control groups, for a total of 530 units. We suggest that a possible explanation for the higher number of pairs within the French sample lies in the fact that news coverage tends to be more geographically concentrated, focusing on Quebec and giving less space and airtime to news from other provinces: the result is a smaller "news universe," and papers and TV are more likely to select the same stories for coverage.

Below, we will present tables showing the similarity levels for English and French media for each of the five story elements: leads, dimensions, language, sources and spin, in addition to the "index score" for test and control groups. Our hypothesis points to greater levels of similarity for the test than for the control groups in both English and French media; however, the literature raised doubts that we would be able to find support for this hypothesis.

Story Leads

For story leads, we found different levels of similarity in the English (Table 3.2A) and French media (Table 3.2B), but in both cases a relatively small proportion (12.2 per cent Eng., 23.4 per cent Fr.) of the identified pairs were considered "very similar." In the French-language sample, two-thirds (66.6 per cent) of the pairs had "somewhat similar" leads, compared to fewer than half (40.9 per cent) of the English pairs. The difference between the test and control pairs is not statistically significant for the English sample, so that the slightly greater proportion of "very similar" leads in the control pairs is likely due to chance variation. However, in the French sample, there is some support for the hypothesis, as 29.8 per cent of the test pairs were "very similar," compared to 20.1 per cent of the control pairs. Although this finding is statistically significant, the relationship between ownership and lead similarity is rather weak (Phi and Cramer's V tests were used here due to asymmetrical results). Since the proportion of "somewhat similar" pairs is higher in the control group (69.9 per cent compared to 60.2 per cent for the test group), the percentages of "very different" pairs are virtually identical in the test and control groups.

Story Dimensions

For story dimensions, the largest group of pairs were seen to be "somewhat similar"—62.2 per cent (Eng.) and 49.3 per cent (Fr.). The "very similar" percentage is overall quite low—13.5 per cent (Eng.) and 15.1 per cent (Fr.). The French-language sample (Table 3.3B) shows a higher number of "very similar" pairs in the test group (17.9 per cent versus 13.6 per cent for the control group), and, as for story leads, this finding is statistically significant, but again the relationship between ownership and similarity of story dimensions (Cramer's V = 0.129) is weak, as the French test group also shows a higher proportion of "very different" pairs than the control group.

In the English-language sample, again there is a statistically significant relationship; however, it was among the control group pairs that the higher level of similar story dimensions was found, both for "very" and for "somewhat similar" pairs. After reviewing the similar pairs, we suggest that the substantive explanation for this unexpected finding does not involve convergence-inspired content-sharing between CBC's *The National* and the two independently owned newspapers. Instead, the similarity within control group pairs appears to be a consequence of both the CBC and the control newspapers subscribing to The Canadian Press (CP) newswire. For example, for the CBC/*Chronicle*

TABLE 3.3A Story Dimension Similarity, by Test and Control Groups (English)

	TEST		CONTROL		TOTAL	
	N	%	N	%	N	%
Rather different	68	29.2	42	19.2	110	24.3
Somewhat similar	139	59.7	142	64.8	28	62.2
Very similar	26	11.2	35	16.0	61	13.5
Total	233	100.1	219	100.0	451	100.0

x^2 = 7.079 df = 2 Sig. = .029 Phi =.125 Cramer's V = .125

TABLE 3.3B Story Dimension Similarity, by Test and Control Groups (French)

	TEST		CONTRÔLE		TOTAL	
	N	%	N	%	N	%
Plutôt différent	72	41.6	105	32.4	177	35.6
Assez semblable	70	40.5	175	54.0	245	49.3
Très semblable	31	17.9	44	13.6	75	15.1
Total	173	100.0	324	100.0	497	100.0

x^2 = 8.294 df = 2 Sig. = .016 Phi = .129 Cramer's V = .129

Herald comparison, among the pairs, overall a fifth (21.6 per cent) of the newspaper's stories came from the CP wire (the latter data not shown in tabular form).[2]

Story Language

For the English media, the first evidence of possible content-sharing, or at least cooperation among newsrooms of convergent media, is seen in the use of language in stories. As shown in Table 3.4A, the test group had 8.6 per cent of pairs with "very similar" language compared to only 1.8 per cent for the control group; analogous figures for "rather different" language are 54.1 per cent for the test group compared to 67.1 per cent for the control group. These results are statistically significant, indicating that the differences between the control and test groups are not due to chance variation. Nonetheless, the relationship between language and ownership is rather weak (Phi = .177). While there were only four instances where the control group pairs had "very similar" language, there were also relatively few cases among the test pairs (N = 20), for a total of 24 cases of "very similar" language out of 452 pairs.

TABLE 3.4A Language Similarity, by Test and Control Groups (English)

	TEST		CONTROL		TOTAL	
	N	%	N	%	N	%
Rather different	126	54.1	147	67.1	273	60.5
Somewhat similar	87	37.3	68	31.1	155	34.3
Very similar	20	8.6	4	1.8	24	5.3
Total	233	100.0	219	100.0	452	100.1

x^2 = 14.191 df = 2 Sig. = .001 Phi = .177 Cramer's V = .177

TABLE 3.4B Language Similarity, by Test and Control Groups (French)

	TEST		CONTRÔLE		TOTAL	
	N	%	N	%	N	%
Plutôt différent	115	80.4	223	77.4	338	78.4
Assez semblable	22	15.4	59	20.5	81	18.8
Très semblable	6	4.2	6	2.1	12	2.8
Total	143	100.0	288	100.0	431	100.0

x^2 = 2.964 df = 2 n.s.

Even fewer occurrences of "very similar" language use were observed in the French media: only 12 pairs (2.8 per cent) of total pairs, with six for the test group (4.2 per cent) and six for the control group (2.1 per cent). These results are not statistically significant.

Story Sources

Fewer than 5 per cent of the total story pairs in English had used "very similar" sources (Table 3.5A). Instead, for the most part, the sources used in the paired stories were "rather different" (65.2 per cent), while 30.3 per cent were considered to have used "somewhat similar" sources. As hypothesized, the test group pairs did feature more "very similar" sources (5.2 per cent compared with 4.1 per cent for the control group pairs) and concomitantly fewer had "rather different" sources (61.8 per cent versus 68.5 per cent). These differences between English test and control group pairs are not statistically significant, nor are they significant in the French-language sample. Here, however, a greater proportion of "very similar" use of sources was found in the French control group (24.1 per cent of pairs compared to 15.9 per cent for the test group), which runs opposite to our hypothesis.

TABLE 3.5A Source Similarity, by Test and Control Groups (English)

	TEST		CONTROL		TOTAL	
	N	%	N	%	N	%
Rather different	144	61.8	150	68.5	294	65.2
Somewhat similar	77	33.0	60	27.4	137	30.3
Very similar	12	5.2	9	4.1	21	4.6
Total	233	100.0	219	100.0	452	100.1

$x^2 = 2.229$ df = 2 n.s.

TABLE 3.5B Source Similarity, by Test and Control Groups (French)

	TEST		CONTRÔLE		TOTAL	
	N	%	N	%	N	%
Plutôt différent	76	57.6	117	53.2	193	54.8
Assez semblable	35	26.5	50	22.7	85	24.1
Très semblable	21	15.9	53	24.1	74	21.0
Total	132	100.0	220	100.0	352	99.9

$x^2 = 3.408$ df = 2 n.s.

Editorial Direction

For the editorial spin variable, on the English side we find a situation similar to the one we saw with respect to story dimensions—greater similarity in the control group (16.2 per cent) versus 10.4 per cent in the test group (Table 3.6A and B). As previously, the explanation for this lies in the use of wire service copy. Results for the French media are almost identical for the test and control groups, indicating no influence of ownership on editorial evaluation.

In Table 3.7, the editorial spin similarity is shown separately for the four pairings that make up the English test and control groups. There are some interesting differences between CTVglobemedia and Canwest Global. While for CTVglobemedia only 2.6 per cent of pairs contained "very similar" editorial spins, for Canwest this figure is 21.2 per cent. At the same time, however, Canwest had a higher percentage of pairs where the coders detected "no spin"—19.8 per cent as opposed to just 8.7 per cent of pairs for CTVglobemedia (see the last row in Table 3.7 in italics)

There appears to be a paradox here. On the one hand, Canwest story pairs were more likely to offer "very similar" editorial spins than were those of CTVglobemedia for story pairs where spin was detected. Yet on

TABLE 3.6A Editorial "Spin" Similarity, by Test and Control Groups (English)

	TEST		CONTROL		TOTAL	
	N	%	N	%	N	%
Rather different	92	45.8	78	52.7	170	48.7
Somewhat similar	88	43.8	46	31.1	134	38.4
Very similar	21	10.4	24	16.2	45	12.9
Total	201	100.0	148	100.0	349	100.0

$x^2 = 6.621$ df = 2 Sig. = .036 Phi = .138 Cramer's V = .138

TABLE 3.6B Editorial "Spin" Similarity, by Test and Control Groups (French)

	TEST		CONTRÔLE		TOTAL	
	N	%	N	%	N	%
Plutôt différent	105	71.9	180	74.1	285	73.3
Assez semblable	31	21.2	52	21.4	83	21.3
Très semblable	10	6.8	11	4.5	21	5.4
Total	146	100.0	243	100.0	389	100.0

$x^2 = .970$ df = 2 n.s.

the other hand, Canwest story pairs were less likely to contain any editorial evaluation compared to those of its corporate competitor. At first blush, our search for an explanation for this focused on the possibility that Canwest's corporate ideology, made very explicit in its 2001–2002 series of national editorials (see Soderlund and Hildebrandt, 2005: 114–119), had indeed filtered down to individual journalists, either through the hiring process, or due to an understanding on the part of journalists as to what their owners' positions on various issues might be. However, a closer examination of Canwest's "very similar" pairs (to be discussed later in the chapter) failed to confirm this explanation. In any case, given the higher level of Canwest pairs with no detectable spin, as well as the fact that the percentage of Canwest's "very similar" pairs registered only just over the two CBC/newspaper control groups (21.2 per cent compared to 15.2 per cent and 17.4 per cent), this suggests that CTV-globemedia's low 2.6 per cent of "similar pairs" is the exception to be explained, not the relatively similar results for the other groups.

TABLE 3.7   Editorial "Spin" Similarity, by Individual Media Groups (English)

	CTVglobemedia		Canwest Global		CBC-HCH		CBC-WFP		TOTAL	
	N	%	N	%	N	%	N	%	N	%
Rather different	56	48.3	36	42.4	45	57.0	33	47.8	170	48.7
Somewhat similar	57	49.1	31	36.5	22	27.8	24	34.8	134	38.4
Very similar	3	2.6	18	21.2	12	15.2	12	17.4	45	12.9
Total	116	100.0	85	101.1	79	100.0	69	100.0	349	100.0
No spin code*	11	8.7	21	19.8	46	36.8	25	26.6	103	22.8

x^2 = 23.403 df = 6 Sig. = .001 Phi = .259 Cramer's V = .183

*Note: The number of cases without a coded spin is not included in the total row.

Index of Similarity Scores

To assess the overall similarity of stories in media pairs, we constructed a "similarity score index" by calculating the average of all five similarity scores. This result was then recoded into three levels, to parallel the original similarity scores. The range from one to three was divided into three equal parts: 1 to 1.66—"rather different," 1.67 to 2.33—"somewhat similar" and 2.34 to 3—"very similar."[3]

When all the similarity scores are combined in this index, we can see from Table 3.8A that there is little evidence overall of content-sharing among either test or control group pairs in the English-language media, as just over 6 per cent of the overall sample produced a "very similar" index score, while one-third of the pairs (32.7 per cent) were considered "somewhat similar" across all dimensions. For the French sample, the combination of all similarity scores as shown in Table 3.8B yields almost identical results for test and control groups. For both languages, well over half of the coverage of the pairs (61.1 per cent Eng., 56.7 per cent Fr.) was in fact "rather different."

Discussion

The results of our study produced little evidence that in 2007 overt content-sharing was taking place in the newsrooms of cross-owned

TABLE 3.8A Index Similarity, by Test and Control Groups (English)

	TEST		CONTROL		TOTAL	
	N	%	N	%	N	%
Rather different	136	58.4	140	63.9	276	61.1
Somewhat similar	82	35.2	66	30.1	148	32.7
Very similar	15	6.4	13	5.9	28	6.2
Total	233	100.0	219	99.9	452	100.0

$x^2 = 1.469\ df = 2$ n.s.

TABLE 3.8B Index Similarity, by Test and Control Groups (French)

	TEST		CONTRÔLE		TOTAL	
	N	%	N	%	N	%
Plutôt différent	98	55.7	183	57.2	281	56.7
Assez semblable	65	36.9	113	35.3	178	35.9
Très semblable	13	7.4	24	7.5	37	7.5
Total	176	100.0	320	100.0	496	100.1

$x^2 = .130\ df = 2$ n.s.

Canadian media companies.[4] In the French-language sample, the test pairs were more often "very similar" in their story leads and story dimensions, while English cross-owned media appeared more similar on the language indicator. All of these findings showed weak relationships, at best, between ownership and content similarity. In addition, the English sample yielded two instances of statistical significance where the non-cross-owned control group showed the greater similarity (story dimensions and spin).

On the overall *index score*, a majority of pairs were considered "rather different" (61.1 per cent Eng., 56.7 per cent Fr.), while few story pairs (6.2 per cent Eng., 7.5 per cent Fr.) were considered "very similar." In addition, even the relatively small amount of "very similar" content found in both test and control groups appears to be accounted for by three factors not related to ownership convergence: the nature of the news event itself, a common reliance on wire services and/or the use of press releases/press conferences as the basis for the news reports, and, to a more limited extent, "pack journalism."

Some similarity in story leads at TVA/*Journal de Montréal* may be explained by a common news culture leaning toward "tabloid-style" journalism. For example, the accidental death of a school bus driver on Montreal's South Shore was covered extensively by the Quebecor media, using very similar story dimensions and sources, including interviews with children who were on the bus at the time of the accident. Interestingly, a weekly Quebecor opinion poll generally produced fairly different coverage on TV than in the newspaper. While this seems to lend credence to the idea that convergence can in fact lead to complementary rather than redundant content, upon closer analysis, we found that if we had taken visuals (in this case, graphics) into account, the similarity score would have been higher.

Stories that focused on national and international events exhibited the highest level of content similarity. For example, stories dealing with a US troop surge in Iraq, the possible extradition of a Russian spy to Great Britain, charges laid by the RCMP in the "Income Trust Scandal," fallout from a provincial election in Quebec, a memorial to fallen firefighters in Winnipeg, and the controversy over "veiled voting" in Federal elections—stories often based on one or more of wire services, press releases, press conferences, testimony and/or scrums—tended to show the most similarities in content. At the same time, a careful re-examination of these story pairs failed to point to direct content-sharing on the part of the newsrooms involved.

A legitimate question to ask is what accounts for the similarity, albeit extremely small, in the English control pairs? Common reliance on the CP wire appears to be the explanation. In every case we examined in detail, the CBC filed full stories with CBC reporters, but it appears that the impetus for coverage and the sources used in the stories came from the wire service. For example, in February 2007 both the Halifax *Chronicle-Herald* and the *Winnipeg Free Press* ran a CP story on workplace violence. The study was released by Statistics Canada and all the media accounts were based on statistics related to violence in the workplace and also featured the same source from the Canadian Initiative on Workplace Violence to comment on the findings. Despite these similarities, a close examination of the reports shows that while the CBC's *The National* reporter may have based her report on the CP story, she nonetheless obtained her own on-camera interviews. In this case, while the content was highly similar, the story was nevertheless clearly treated independently by the three news organizations (CBC, the Halifax *Chronicle-Herald* and the *Winnipeg Free Press*). Other highly similar stories involved findings of a study showing that naps are good for the heart and a story on banks having to issue new credit cards due to theft of computer data. In both cases, the television reporter filed a complete report with on-camera interviews. Any similarity in content was due to the nature of the original news releases, with information being reported without much treatment or spin. In the French media, all news outlets showed abundant use of CP material; in one case, a story lead read by TVA anchor Sophie Thibault (about Pauline Marois's bid for leadership of the Parti Québécois) was copied verbatim from the CP story.

Among the English test group pairs there were relatively few CTVglobemedia stories that were considered "very similar." One of these is the account of the death of Corporal Matthew McCully in Afghanistan. In addition to the use of the identical quote from Col. Mike Cessford, "We lost a good kid today" (which can be attributed to "pack journalism"), the story leads were similar, and, in addition to Col. Cessford, Chief of Defence Staff General Rick Hillier was quoted in both stories, although the quotes used from General Hillier were different. Foreign policy analyst Norine MacDonald was interviewed for the television story, while Lt. Col. Rob Walker and Prime Minister Stephen Harper were quoted in the newspaper account. Story dimensions covered were also similar—an explanation of the mission on which McCully was killed, the strategy of cooperation with Afghan military units, and the voicing of skepticism regarding the ultimate success of the mission.

A second CTVglobemedia "very similar" story pair focused on the grounding for inspection of Bombardier Q400 turboprop aircraft following a series of landing gear failures in Europe. In this case the story leads were similar—the plane crashes and the resulting public relations nightmare for Bombardier—as were the story dimensions—the landing gear mishaps causing the planes to crash, the Scandinavian Airlines decision to ground its entire fleet of Q400s, Bombardier's need to move quickly to restore confidence in the aircraft, and reports that the Canadian carrier, Porter Airlines, was not grounding its Q400 aircraft. Sources used in the stories were similar as well—Bombardier, Transport Canada, Porter Airlines, and industry experts—but in this case the actual spokespersons were different. However, the editorial spin was similar—that in spite of its current problems, the Q400 was a safe aircraft and that Bombardier would "get it right." While both *Global National* and the *National Post* covered the story for Canwest, the television account was only a brief 20–30 second summary of the event, which made any detailed comparison of the story pair impossible. Interestingly, however, the *National Post* account was very similar to that which appeared in the *Globe and Mail*, with the word "upstart" used to describe Porter Airlines in both stories, when one might have thought that a better word choice would have been "start-up."

Among the Canwest story pairs that received a high similarity score was the report on the RCMP findings on the "Liberal Income Trust Scandal." The fact that the RCMP exonerated the Liberal Government provided the story lead and led to a similar editorial spin on the part of *Global National* and *National Post* stories—that only a single bureaucrat working in the Department of Finance, Serge Nadeau, had been charged with breach of trust, but that the Liberals were not likely to be on the receiving end of a series of apologies any time soon. As well, the stories were considered similar because both provided background to the original scandal and both reported that no politician was implicated in the alleged leak of information prior to the budget announcement that income trusts would not be taxed. Sources used in the stories were also similar: RCMP Chief Superintendent Dan Killam, Ralph Goodale and Jim Flaherty appeared prominently in both stories. It is difficult to conclude, however, that the two reporters might have shared sources or cooperated on the story as the sources, as well as the quotes from Killam, came from the media briefing announcing the charges, while those from Goodale and Flaherty came from comments made in scrums in the House of Commons available to all media. As well, there were sources unique to each story; for the television story, Stephen Harper, Stéphane Dion and MP Mark Holland appeared, while in the newspaper account, Mr. Nadeau's lawyer, Raphael Schacter, was interviewed.

Another domestic political issue, the controversy over "veiled voting" by Muslim women, led to "very similar" pairs in both the French test (TVA/*Journal de Montréal*) and control groups (SRC/*La Presse*, SRC/*Le Devoir*), as well as in the Canwest media. This issue surfaced when Elections Canada announced that in three upcoming Quebec by-elections Muslim women would be allowed to vote without having to show their faces; while Elections Canada saw no problem with the practice, Prime Minister Harper thought otherwise. In the context of the "reasonable accommodations" debate in Quebec, all French media ran extensive coverage of this story over several days. In some stories where *Global National*/*National Post* or TVA/*Journal de Montréal* showed similar treatment, content was considered similar in other news outlets as well.

In light of earlier national editorial positions, one might have thought that Canwest would have taken a corporate position on this issue. *Global National* and *National Post* story leads were in fact similar in the way the story was framed; as well, the story dimensions covered were similar—the genesis of the problem (a new Elections Act, Bill C-31), the context (the debate over "reasonable accommodation" to minority practices in Quebec), Elections Canada's position, Mr. Harper's position, and the views of Canada's Muslim community. Only Mr. Harper, however, appeared as a source in both stories. In the *Global National* story, Chief Electoral Officer Marc Mayrand spoke for Elections Canada, while in the newspaper story this role was performed by John Enright. On television, the views of the Muslim community were put forward by Sarah El Gazzar from the Canadian Council of American-Islamic Relations, while Mohamed Elmasry from the Canadian Islamic Congress and Alia Hogben from the Canadian Council of Canadian Women were interviewed for the newspaper article. The editorial spin was similar, but it was not the one that might have been expected; the spin was that the "problem" of veiled voting was created for political gain by the prime minister, because showing their faces while casting a ballot had not been an issue for Muslim women in the past, nor was it an issue now.

A story that bridged national and international politics, Canada's negative vote on a UN Universal Declaration of Indigenous Peoples' Rights, also occasioned a "very similar" pair of Canwest stories. In this case, both story leads stressed the paradox of Canada, a country noted for its record of supporting human rights, having refused to cast a vote in favour of the widely supported (143 to four) declaration. Story dimensions were also similar—a discussion of the provisions of the declaration, reasons for Canada's refusal to vote for it, and negative reactions from Canada's Aboriginal community. In addition, the newspaper story dealt with the "politics of passage" at the UN, a dimension not covered on TV. Interestingly, while the sources used in the two stories differed completely, the editorial spin was quite similar—by siding with the United States, Australia and New Zealand in voting against the majority of world opinion, Canada had created alienation in its Aboriginal community and risked embarrassment at the international level.

The testimony of General David Petraeus before the US Congress in September 2007 is the final "very similar" internationally focused Canwest story pair that we will discuss in detail. In this case, story leads were based on the general's assessment that the "troop surge" undertaken earlier in the year to curb violence in Iraq "was working." Story dimensions were also similar—the positive effects of the troop surge, the questioning of this conclusion by critics, and the consequences of an early troop withdrawal. Both stories quoted General Petraeus and US Ambassador to Iraq Ryan Crocker in support of the Bush Administration's Iraq strategy. In the TV story, criticism came in the form of interjections by Democratic detractors, while in the newspaper account skepticism on the part of Congressman Tom Lantos was quoted, while the arguments of the protest groups Code Pink and Moveon.org were summarized. The editorial spin in the two stories was similar—there was little optimism for an early or successful end to the war and the Bush Administration was in for a tough sell to the American people.

It is important to point out that it is difficult to link any of these editorial evaluations to the "core positions" put forward in Canwest's earlier series of national editorials, which, on the domestic side, generally supported "small government," and specifically a "flat tax" and a "Triple-E Senate," while on the international side, they condemned terrorism and voiced unequivocal support for Israel in its struggle with Palestinian leader Yasser Arafat (Soderlund and Hildebrandt, 2005: 118–119).

Yet another factor leading us to conclude that similarities in Canwest story pairs were not due to content-sharing is that in some stories where *Global National* and the *National Post* showed very similar treatment, content was also considered very similar in other news outlets. For example, coverage of the anniversary of the Dawson College shooting was also considered very similar in the control pair consisting of CBC's *The National* and the *Winnipeg Free Press*. There was also a short anchor-only story on compensation for victims of "agent orange" that was similar for both *Global National* and the *National Post*. In this case, it appears that both news outlets were simply providing a brief update based on a government-issued press release. Consequently, the CBC, Canwest and CTVglobemedia all covered the story in roughly the same, albeit brief, manner. (The control group newspapers did not cover the story).

As noted above, the stories that were most likely to have similar content for both the test and control pairs dealt with national topics, with the second highest category focusing on international events—precisely the types of stories that are most likely to involve wire service coverage. The use of wire services as a means to homogenize news has been a long-standing and well-documented practice. Scholars like Debra Clarke argue that the use of newswires "represents a well-entrenched form of convergence that has long resulted in the cross-media content duplication of international news." She adds that "[a]mong Canadian news organizations, extensive use of Canadian Press (CP) news agency as a historically pivotal source has assured the same results in the production of national news" (2005: 167). Thus, what we observed in this study is less that convergence has resulted in more news sharing (as clearly it has not), but rather that the previous practices of reliance on newswires and pack journalism continued much as before.

Conclusion

As our study looked only at "old" media (television and newspapers), we did not test for the second stage of convergence—that of "cloning" content for use on the Internet. However, we did fail to find evidence of coopetition, as newspaper journalists did not appear on television and television reporters did not write for newspapers in any of our sample weeks. In fact, of the few instances where there was similarity in content or sources, we found that the non-ownership-connected control groups showed about as much similarity as did the cross-owned test groups. Moreover, these similarities were not due to actual content-sharing, but rather to the nature of the news events themselves and/or reliance on a common third source such as wire services or press releases, press conferences and/or scrums.

Surprisingly, none of the stories examined had links to additional information to be found on company websites, nor did any journalists encourage viewers or readers to obtain more information from a partner news agency within the corporation. Indeed, the only mention of corporate websites was seen on television where at the end of the newscast, as in the case of *Global National*, audiences were encouraged to stream the program or download a podcast of the program. For CBC, there were promotions telling viewers to go to the cbc.ca website for "news at anytime," as well as promotions of CBC radio and television's *Newsworld*. These promotional comments always came at the very end of the newscast and were not associated with any particular story. For CTV, the corporate website was only mentioned on Fridays, when viewers were encouraged to send their comments on the newscasts to either a mailing address or ctv.ca.

4
Content-Sharing in English-Language Local Market Media

Introduction

THE QUESTION WE ADDRESS in this chapter is whether the conclusions showing the lack of content-sharing at the "national" level as reported in the previous chapter are replicated with respect to news production at the "local market" level. Specifically, while Canadian media giants appear to have been unable to implement convergence practices among their flagship properties, might we have looked in the wrong place to see the impact of content-sharing? For example, Kyle Geissler has reported that "smaller markets prove to be a fertile ground for newsroom convergence because of their small size, versatility and need to economize resources" (2006: v). Therefore, was it among local-market television newsrooms that content-sharing had managed to achieve a greater level of operational success? After all, local markets are perhaps where economic pressure is less intense; the logistics of implementation are less complex; and the journalists are younger, more recent graduates of journalism schools and/or their egos are smaller. The Edmonton comparison was chosen in part because Canwest appeared to have jumped on the convergence bandwagon earlier than its competitors (Dacruz, 2004, Mar. 25), and in part because Canwest's Edmonton television channel was available to us by way of satellite transmission.

TABLE 4.1   Story Lead Similarity, by Local Test and Selected Control Groups

Story Lead Similarity	Edmonton: Edmonton Journal & Global Edmonton's News Hour		National: National Post & Global National		Control: Halifax CH, Winnipeg FP & CBC's The National	
	N	%	N	%	N	%
Very different	68	50.7	42	39.6	107	48.9
Somewhat similar	54	40.3	48	45.3	84	38.4
Very similar	12	9.0	16	15.1	28	12.8
Total	134	100.0	106	100.0	219	100.1

$x^2 = 4.564$ df = 4 ns

TABLE 4.2   Story Dimension Similarity, by Local Test and Selected Control Groups

Story Dimension Similarity	Edmonton: Edmonton Journal & Global Edmonton's News Hour		National: National Post & Global National		Control: Halifax CH, Winnipeg FP & CBC's The National	
	N	%	N	%	N	%
Very different	30	22.2	37	34.9	42	19.2
Somewhat similar	82	60.7	55	51.9	142	64.8
Very similar	23	17.0	14	13.2	35	16.0
Total	135	99.9	106	100.0	219	100.0

$x^2 = 10.93$ df = 4 Sig. = .037 Phi = .149 Cramer's V = .105

Findings

For the local market study, story pairs from Edmonton Global's major evening newscast, *The News Hour,* and Canwest's daily newspaper, the *Edmonton Journal,* were compared with Canwest's national television-newspaper data, as well as control data from the two CBC/newspaper control groups, both used in the previous chapter. Once more we used similarity scores for paired TV/newspaper stories on five elements of similarity, as well as a similarity index that combines all five elements.

Table 4.1 shows the extent of similarity in story leads. While the results are not statistically significant, we find that Canwest's local media properties, counter to our hypothesis, showed the lowest number of "very similar" pairs (9.0 per cent), while its national properties showed the greatest amount (15.1 per cent); the national control group occupied a

TABLE 4.3   Story Language Similarity, by Test and Selected Control Groups

Story Language Similarity	Edmonton: *Edmonton Journal* & Global Edmonton's *News Hour*		National: *National Post* & *Global National*		Control: Halifax *CH*, Winnipeg *FP* & CBC's *The National*	
	N	%	N	%	N	%
Very different	51	40.5	53	50.0	147	67.1
Somewhat similar	68	54.0	43	40.6	68	31.1
Very similar	7	5.6	10	9.4	4	1.8
Total	126	100.1	106	100.0	219	100.0

x^2 = 30.7, df = 4 Sig. < .000 Phi = .261 Cramer's V = .185

middle position (12.8 per cent). In addition, Canwest's Edmonton-based properties showed the greatest amount of "very different" pairs (50.7 per cent), while its national properties showed the least amount (39.6 per cent), and the control group again occupied the middle ground. Note that the percentage of "very different" pairs surpassed those coded "very similar" by substantial margins in all three conditions.

With respect to story dimensions, with results statistically significant at the .05 level, in Table 4.2 we see the first evidence that convergence effects might be stronger at the local level. Canwest's Edmonton media produced the greatest amount of "very similar" pairs (17.0 per cent), ahead of Canwest's national media at 13.2 per cent. The national control group again occupied the middle position, with 16.0 per cent of its story pairs coded as "very similar." On this content-sharing indicator, by far the largest group of pairs were seen to be "somewhat similar"—over half for all groups studied. While the x^2 statistic indicates that the results are not due to chance, the Cramer's V statistic, which measures the strength of the relationship (.105), is very weak.

With results significant at the .000 level, as with story leads, data in Table 4.3 tell us that with respect to story language it was Canwest's national media that again evidenced the greatest amount of "very similar" pairs (9.4 per cent), followed by its Edmonton media (5.6 per cent) and the control group at 1.8 per cent. However, the local Edmonton Canwest properties were considerably more likely to use "somewhat" or "very" similar language than either of the other groups: 5.6 per cent + 54.0 per cent = 59.6 per cent, compared with 9.4 per cent + 40.6 per cent = 50 per cent for Canwest national, and 1.8 per cent + 31.1 per cent = 32.9 per cent for the national control group.

TABLE 4.4   Story Source Similarity, by Local Test and Selected Control Groups

Story Source Similarity	Edmonton: Edmonton Journal & Global Edmonton's News Hour		National: National Post & Global National		Control: Halifax CH, Winnipeg FP & CBC's The National	
	N	%	N	%	N	%
Very different	63	48.8	71	67.0	150	68.5
Somewhat similar	36	27.9	29	27.4	60	27.4
Very similar	30	23.3	6	5.7	9	4.1
Total	135	100.0	106	100.1	219	100.0

$x^2 = 38.0$ df = 4 Sig. < .001 Phi = .289 Cramer's V = .205

As seen in Table 4.4, on the similarity indicator of common sources used, we find more evidence that convergence may indeed have had greater success at the local level. With findings significant at the .001 level, Edmonton-based media produced almost a quarter of "very similar" story pairs (23.3 per cent), with just over another quarter coded as "somewhat similar," and only 48.8 percent being "very different." Canwest's national media trailed by almost 20 per cent in terms of "very similar" pairs (5.7 per cent), while showing the same amount of "somewhat similar" pairs, but almost 20 per cent more "very different" pairs. The control group, while also showing just over a quarter of story pairs using "somewhat similar" sources, had only 4.1 per cent using "very similar" sources, and the highest level of "very different" sources (68.5 per cent). Clearly, local journalists working in both television and print were far less likely than their national counterparts to seek out alternative sources. While this could be seen as an indicator of source-sharing, in our discussion below we will offer a different and more plausible explanation for this finding.

With the caveat that only 20 of 135 Edmonton-based story pairs could be coded for spin, and with results nowhere near statistical significance, it is hard to make too much of the fact that our hypothesized relationship is again reflected in the data shown in Table 4.5. Nevertheless, Canwest's local Edmonton-based media produced 35.0 per cent "very similar" story pairs (N = 7), its national media 21.2 per cent (N = 18), while the national control group placed only 16.2 per cent (N = 24) in the "very similar" category.

To assess the overall similarity of stories in story pairs, we used the same "similarity score index" as employed in chapter 3, by calculating

TABLE 4.5 Story "Spin" Similarity, by Local Test and Selected Control Groups**

Story Spin Similarity	Edmonton: Edmonton Journal & Global Edmonton's News Hour		National: National Post & Global National		Control: Halifax CH, Winnipeg FP & CBC's The National	
	N	%	N	%	N	%
Very different	7	35.0	36	42.4	78	52.7
Somewhat similar	6	30.0	31	36.5	46	31.1
Very similar	7	35.0	18	21.2	24	16.2
Total	20	100.0	85	100.1	148	100.0

$x^2 = 5.9$ df = 4 ns

**This variable has far more missing data than the other similarity variables, because for many stories no spin could be detected, and thus no similarity of spin was coded. Due to the factual nature of local stories, this was especially true for stories in the Edmonton media.

TABLE 4.6 Overall Similarity Index, by Local Test and Selected Control Groups

Similarity Index	Edmonton: Edmonton Journal & Global Edmonton's News Hour		National: National Post & Global National		Control: Halifax CH, Winnipeg FP & CBC's The National	
	N	%	N	%	N	%
Very different	65	48.1	57	53.8	141	63.9
Somewhat similar	61	45.2	39	36.8	65	30.1
Very similar	9	6.7	10	9.4	13	5.9
Total	135	100.0	106	100.0	219	99.9

$x^2 = 10.4$ df = 4 Sig. < .034 Phi = .151 Cramer's V = 106

the average of all five indicator similarity scores. This result was then recoded into three levels, to parallel the original similarity scores. As for the national results, the range from one to three was divided into three equal parts: 1 to 1.66—"rather different," 1.67 to 2.33—"somewhat similar" and 2.34 to 3—"very similar."

When all the similarity indicator scores are combined in this index (Table 4.6), on the one hand, Canwest's national media showed the greatest amount of high content similarity (9.4 per cent), with its Edmonton properties occupying a mid-position (6.7 per cent) and the national control group showing just under 6 per cent of "very similar" story pairs. In addition, the share of "very different" story pairs is lowest in the Edmonton local media (48.1 per cent), higher in the Canwest pairings, and shows the greatest variety across properties for the control group (63.9 per cent). While the strength of these findings is weak, they are statistically significant at the .05 level, indicating the likely absence of a chance occurrence. On the other hand, we must point out that even Canwest's national percentage of 9.4 accounts for less than 10 per cent of total content and that its Edmonton percentage of 6.7 per cent is virtually identical to the average of 6.2 per cent recorded for all national media studied (see chapter 3, Table 3.8A, this volume).

What are we to make of these findings? Clearly, our hypothesis that convergence effects would more likely be seen at the local level was not summarily confirmed, although similarities were significantly greater for the Edmonton-based test group on language, sources and spin, and even on the overall index. But what accounts for both Canwest's national and local media showing a greater amount of convergence effects than the non-ownership-connected control group? Can this really be attributed to content-sharing?

Explanations for content similarities between Canwest national television and newspaper properties as well as those in the control groups were advanced in chapter 3 and we will not review them here. However, we will explore below the reasons for similarities between Canwest's Edmonton-based media. "Very similar" pairs are primarily of two types, resulting in relatively brief and fact-based accounts of events on television as well as in the newspaper.

First, stories from Edmonton and the surrounding local area included reports of homicides, shootings, traffic accidents, drug raids and fires. These stories often cited the same police or fire spokespersons as sources, thus accounting for the relatively high percentage of stories with "very similar" sources. For example, a pair of stories in January 2007 reported the discovery of two unconscious men, one of whom later died and whose death was deemed a homicide. Both stories were based on police reports and contained "very similar" leads, language and sources. Later that same year, a May accident in Evansburg, Alberta, involving a semi-trailer plunging off a bridge into the Pembina River, and the September death of a British soldier in an off-duty skydiving accident in southern Alberta received similar summary treatment in both TV and newspaper reporting. Another pair of stories reporting a drugs and weapons raid in December cited the same two police sources (Sergeant Daren Derko and Inspector Gerry Gunn), although in this case somewhat different quotes from the officers were used in the paired stories. Beyond individual journalists' contacts and who was reachable on a given day, the choice of sources no doubt reflects institutional norms with respect to who are considered competent and reliable sources for particular kinds of stories. As well, relatively few of these types of stories had a detectable spin, as they tended to simply report what had occurred, offering little in the way of further elaboration.

Second, "very similar" international story pairs tended to deal with reports summarizing the more "sensational" events in the United States and elsewhere, such as mass shootings in shopping malls, one of which occurred in Omaha, Nebraska, in December 2007, where a teenaged gunman opened fire, killing eight people (newspaper story) or nine people (TV story), or horrendous traffic accidents like the one in Coahuila, Mexico, in September that same year, where a tractor-trailer loaded with explosives crashed into a pickup truck and burst into flames, killing 37 people.

On a number of indicators, stories of a "human interest" nature, wherever they might occur, also contributed to "very similar" coverage. One such story pair dealt with a local competition among Edmonton's "top dogs" for an appearance in a local production of the musical *Oliver*—both TV and newspaper stories used the same sources. Another story pair reported the repatriation of a British schoolteacher, Gillian Gibbons, from Sudan, where she had been pardoned following a jail sentence for allowing her class to name a teddy bear Muhammad. In both the television and newspaper stories, Ms. Gibbons was the sole source of information and the spin was that she had been well-treated.

The only story pair among all those analyzed for both the national and the local media components of the study that we can say with confidence demonstrated content-sharing appeared in the Edmonton-based comparison. The story dealt with automobiles that had been involved in serious crashes and had been bought at salvage auctions in Ontario. Depending on the location of the damage, the front and rear ends from these wrecks were then welded together to form "new" vehicles and brought to Alberta to be sold to unsuspecting buyers in "curbside" transactions.

The television and newspaper stories reporting this scam clearly involved content-sharing. The story originated on Edmonton Global's *News Hour* on February 13, 2007, as an in-depth report by reporter Susan Tymofichuk. Interviewed for the story were Bob Hamilton of the Alberta Motor Vehicle Industry Council as well as Nirmal Singh Bhui, a buyer of such a "repaired" vehicle. The *Edmonton Journal* story appeared a day later, and acknowledged the Global television story as the source. The story was virtually identical to the television version, with the same lead, the same dimensions, the same sources, the same quotes and the same spin—"buyer beware." What is interesting in this case is that the material generated by a Canwest television journalist, although ultimately appearing in another Canwest media property, was not shared directly; the newspaper story that appeared in the *Edmonton Journal*, based on Ms. Tymofichuk's story, was attributed to The Canadian Press wire service.[1] Thus, the auto scam investigation story demonstrates that similar content found in multiple outlets of converged media properties is not necessarily evidence of convergence-inspired content-sharing.

Part II

Canadian Media: Now and into the Future

5

Media Executives Assess the Impact of Convergence and New Media

Background

IN THE SECOND PHASE OF OUR RESEARCH, between the spring of 2009 and the winter of 2010, we contacted executives of the three major media companies studied, as well as those representing all the specific media platforms included in our study. In total, eight responded positively to our request for interviews: five representing English-language and three representing French-language media companies. In this phase of the study, our goal was to be able to offer readers a comprehensive picture of where Canadian media stood, not only with respect to the impact of cross-ownership but more generally where executives believed both newspaper and television industries were headed in the troubled times brought on by the challenge of "new media," and compounded by the crisis that hit world financial markets in the fall of 2008 and blossomed into a full recession in 2009.

We must first point out that, for whatever reason, there was little enthusiasm on the part of media executives to share with us their views on issues of ownership and content-sharing.[1] Executives who agreed to an interview were sent copies of our findings prior to the interviews, and at the beginning of the interviews we asked them for comments or questions on these findings. The major question we then asked of media executives was why the synergies supposed to be achieved by the convergence model had not been realized. Following this, we asked whether convergence was indeed dead or whether, especially in dire financial times, it might take on some new form of life. We ended the interviews with some general questions regarding the future for newspapers and television industries in Canada in light of the problems that have emerged with media and audience fragmentation, the popularization of the Internet, and challenges to the financial underpinnings of their traditional business models.

Points of General Agreement

No executive with whom we spoke found our findings surprising; there was widespread agreement among those we interviewed that television-print content convergence had not happened. Several reasons were mentioned for this, including resistance on the part of journalists (greater in Quebec), inherent difficulties in merging what in effect are two very different styles of journalism, a "silo mentality" on the part of producers and editors, regulatory prohibitions and restrictive union agreements (with respect to Quebecor), and "not really trying too hard" (with respect to Canwest Global).

There was also the expected uncertainty expressed regarding the continued viability of business models in place for both conventional television and print news, although no one saw the situation as catastrophic. In fact, most painted a picture of conditions that were better than one might have expected. Concerns over business models were combined with a universal understanding regarding the necessity to meet the challenges of the Internet—chiefly how to make online products profitable. There was also consensus that "multitasking" and the skills to operate in multiple platforms were a reality for future journalists.

Greater concern was expressed in Quebec that the switch to the use of corporate news service models would lead to more shared content; this was especially the case with respect to the impact of Quebec Media Inc. (QMI, the new Quebecor corporate news service) on Quebecor platforms. Among English Canadian executives, there likewise were concerns expressed over the move to corporate news services, but these concerns centred largely on their impact on The Canadian Press. At least one executive in both official languages expressed concern over the consolidation of *content creation* and *content distribution* under the same ownership, a development we will review in the Postscript to this book. There was also a widespread and deep concern that job cuts had already reduced to near critical levels the ability of Canadian media to gather and report news in a responsible way.

Points of Divergence

English Canadian executives tended not to see content-sharing as constituting a major problem, as limited benefits were perceived to be gained from the practice relative to the effort needed to make it work. It was felt that the future for both newspapers and television lay with the Internet, and that profitable exploitation of their web ventures would be the chief focus of both media in the coming years. Perhaps the most striking feature of this set of interviews was the degree of optimism expressed about pursuing online ventures in what has been widely portrayed as a scenario of gloom (if not doom) for "old" media industries.

Quebec executives focused heavily on regulatory prohibitions and union restrictions as constraints on content-sharing at Quebecor. Content-sharing was seen to have both negative and positive effects. On the negative side, content-sharing within Quebecor (as a result of QMI) and Radio-Canada could be used to permit more newsroom cuts; contrariwise, the more positive effects of convergence could result in the reallocation of resources to produce more original content. Given the lockout at *Le Journal de Montréal* and greater union resistance to joint news-gathering compared to English Canada, any prediction regarding exactly how things would play out in Quebec was seen as difficult.

The government's role as a regulator was also given greater prominence in Quebec. There was also a greater perceived negative impact of cross-ownership on democratic practices, not only because of Quebecor's dominant position in the province, but because of the SRC/Gesca content collaboration following the Quebecor-TVA transaction in 2000.

Executive Interviews

With respect to the findings of the study, a major Canadian newspaper editor offered the view that television-newspaper convergence had been undertaken initially to realize cost savings, but that the realities of journalism were such that in the area of news-gathering, print newsrooms are much stronger than television newsrooms (this was seen to be the case especially with Canwest), and that this made for an asymmetric relationship. In 2007 (at the mid-point of our content analysis study), the move away from CP to a reliance on the Canwest News Service was seen to have resulted from the recognition on the part of management that its print and broadcast properties "had more or less continued to do what they had done previously." Thus, the adoption of what was termed the "corporate news service model" was seen as a new way of achieving cost savings through indirect sharing of content (interview, 2009, Aug. 24).[2] While we have no way of independently verifying whether any savings were realized prior to the breakup of Canwest's TV and newspaper properties, what is clear is that the move to the new news service had led to concerns regarding the future quality of Canadian news overall, as a number of Canwest newspapers pulled their own reporters from both national and provincial press galleries in favour of receiving relevant stories from the corporate news service.[3]

Another concern centred on the consequences of the move for CP. In that Quebecor had indicated its intention to pull out of CP in 2010,[4] not only would there be a diminution of a "strong national voice" (as individual newspapers add content to the newswire as well as take stories from it), there was a real fear for the continued viability of CP itself (interview, 2009, Aug. 24). This concern was reiterated in a number of our interviews.

On the question of the future of Canadian newspapers, one editor self-described as "a huge optimist," and characterized newspapers as "a viable and profitable business." While acknowledging that there would be "a reduction in profit margins from those realized in the past," the editor felt that "the existing business model will prevail," however, in the future newspapers will have "a smaller core audience" (interview, 2009, Aug. 24).

For newspapers, it was felt that the challenge of the Internet will clearly entail "some restructuring to optimize applications on the web." The ongoing search for the "magic bullet," which would enable newspapers to make a profit online, to date had not been fruitful. For example, with respect to providing free online content, the strategy of "growing the audience to attract advertisers" was reported to have been unsuccessful. As a result, some limitation on free content (perhaps restricted to breaking news) was seen as most likely necessary: whatever the ultimate strategy, "newspapers will have to find a way to make money online" (interview, 2009, Aug. 24).

The editor of another major daily newspaper was even more optimistic regarding the future of newspapers, indicating that it was "an exciting time to be in the business." Specifically, the newspaper's website platform opened the possibility for newspapers to abandon the limitations imposed by the daily news cycle and actually run breaking news as fast as radio or television. And, in that newspapers have by far the most news-gatherers, they could do a better job of this than their less well-staffed electronic competitors.

With respect to the Internet, somewhat surprisingly, the editor offered that it was "the best thing that has happened in the last five years." Instead of seeing the web as a competitor, in an era described as "a long, steady transition," the editor believed the Internet should be looked at as something that "needs to be taken advantage of." The editor did acknowledge the problems related to being able to charge for general news content, although it was thought possible to charge for specialty products (interview, 2009, Aug. 26).

Moreover, while online content may not in and of itself be immediately profitable, "huge advantages" were seen as accruing from the Internet, specifically, "the web allows the newspaper to play to the strengths of both hard copy and online; it gives the paper [in its hard copy format] greater visibility and opens a whole new audience to the paper." Particularly cited as critical to being able to attract new audiences were the interactive features of the Internet, with stories run on the web eliciting virtually immediate and often voluminous feedback—a far cry from what in the past had appeared in traditional letters to the editor. Importantly, in this editor's view, in terms of its impact on convergence, the Internet has made redundant the earlier rationale for a newspaper needing to partner with a television station. The editor agreed that corporate news services could be vehicles for greater content-sharing in the future, with both Canwest and Quebecor being big enough to both draw from and add material to such news service networks, with wire services like Reuters, Agence France-Presse, and the *New York Times* service supplying international news (interview, 2009, Aug. 26).

The publisher of a major Canadian newspaper also expressed the view that large-scale sharing of content between television and newspapers was not very likely, given the reality that "TV doesn't generate much content" beyond covering press conferences. It was pointed out that television news tends "to follow the agendas set by others" and plays "virtually no watchdog role." The publisher also questioned whether content-sharing was indeed Canwest's major reason for pulling out of CP in favour of its own news service. He offered that preventing content from falling into the hands of competitors and the high cost of CP content were far more compelling reasons for the change than whatever content might be shared between Canwest's television and newspaper properties. It was his opinion that "CP will survive," but that "its co-op piece will be smaller," with its chief function being "a tip service for breaking news" (interview, 2009, Sept. 1).

As for the future of the newspaper industry itself, the publisher was not nearly as optimistic as the editors with whom we spoke. While he saw the newspaper continuing to survive, he also saw "serious challenges to the business case." These were "an age-related decline in readership" combined with "a more serious decline in advertising revenues," chiefly from losses in classified advertising to the Internet, a trend that has been ongoing since 2000.

In terms of the challenges presented by the Internet to the news-providing function of newspapers, the publisher offered a number of interesting points. First, he did not believe that newspapers could compete with television on the web. Second, he did not see newspaper readers "going elsewhere for news; people are just not attending [to news]." Third, he stressed "the need to understand how people use media," pointing out that "the great bulk of the audience is working during most of the day," which in large measure determines when and how they will access news. The "long-term business case" for newspapers was described as "tough." However, as was the case with the earlier challenge presented by the advent of television, he believed that newspapers would adjust; "there will be a contraction and newspapers will be smaller" (interview, 2009, Sept. 1).

A television executive whom we interviewed offered perhaps the most telling comment regarding why content-sharing was not practiced among Canwest properties—the company simply had not pushed it in a forceful way. While Canwest media platforms were encouraged to "work on projects that made sense" (such as promotions) and "work together to see what you can do," there was "no specific direction" with respect to sharing of content. This was confirmed at a conference panel where our findings were presented in June 2010 when a former Canwest journalist indicated that what sharing of content occurred resulted from informal relationships between reporters. The television executive also agreed with the previous view on the reasons for Canwest's withdrawal from CP, maintaining that the chief reason for the pullout lay not in developing a vehicle for content-sharing, but rather from the problem of having to share content put on the wire "with friends and enemies alike." It was acknowledged, however, that greater internal sharing of content, especially in the area of breaking news, would be a likely outcome of the use of corporate news services (interview, 2009, Aug. 27).

Online products for both newspapers and television were seen to be the major area where the two types of media could achieve the greatest degree of cooperation. It was also suggested that at least some text for both television and newspaper websites would likely come from corporate news services. We asked the executive specifically about the relative advantages of television and newspapers in running a website. The executive felt that TV would feature more extensive video, but would most likely share some of that video with the cross-owned newspaper. As well, with more extensive news-gathering staff, newspapers would be expected to "tip off TV newsrooms to breaking news."

On the question of online newspaper ventures, the TV executive identified the "improvement in websites in dealing with breaking news"—specifically that "newspapers are not holding back content to appear in the printed version of the paper"—as the most significant recent change. For television, as was the case with newspapers, "the use of websites to push people to watch conventional TV news" was seen as a major benefit of online efforts. Again, as with newspapers, it was argued that "in a changing media landscape," at some point "online [efforts] had to turn into money." We queried the executive with respect to the future of conventional local television channels in a 500-channel universe. The response was simple and direct: "[T]he future is news—distinctive local TV news. The only reason local channels exist is local news" (interview, 2009, Aug. 27).

A senior media executive with whom we spoke claimed that not only were "the assumptions going into convergence over-sold, they didn't materialize." Moreover, he maintained that television-newspaper consolidation "doesn't lead to where you think." Specifically, "too much homogenization devalues both [TV and newspaper] products." In fact, content-homogenization was described as being "counter-productive," as market incentives based on consumer preferences called for "the differentiation of products." For multimedia owners, "platform and programming differentiation to consumers" was seen to be the key to success. Also, the reality was that "there were not too many cross-over journalists out there." While "triple-threat journalists" were seen as a rarity, he expected that "the next generation of journalists will be more multidisciplinary" (interview, 2009, Sept. 22).

Whatever content synergies between print and TV were realized came about through changes in technology, which allowed news to be covered with fewer people and produced with greater speed. He saw the future characterized by an increasing reliance on news services, with the question being, "How much unique editorial input would be added?" In terms of content-sharing, he foresaw far greater sharing of both video and audio between platforms within a converged company, as the technology for such sharing is now "far more advanced than previously." He maintained, however, that an entire story "would not be ripped and used"; what would be shared "would be video, with local voice-over presentation" (interview, 2009, Sept. 22).

The future of conventional television was tied to the current "fee for carriage" dispute between conventional broadcasters and cable companies.[5] Two stark options were presented: "an exit from local TV," or a "vertical integration model," wherein the content-producer would also control the pipelines (cable and satellite), as well as Internet sites, newspapers and television networks. In the current environment, this outcome was seen as presenting a far greater concern than that entailed in foreign ownership (interview, 2009, Sept. 22). Of course, both Quebecor and now BCE are configured to exploit the benefits of the vertical integration model.

There appeared to be greater concern among Quebec executives over the impact of cross-ownership on democratic practices than emerged from our English-language interviews. This stemmed not only from Quebecor's dominant position in the province but from the Radio-Canada content collaboration undertaken with Gesca (after Quebecor's acquisition of the TVA network in 2000), an initiative that was not well received in the province. According to a Quebec television executive,

> because of Quebecor specifically, convergence is a huge threat. Not specifically convergence, in fact, but *concentration of information*. I'm not sure people are fully aware of the democratic impact. It's not the role of the media to determine the political agenda of a society. The Liberal Party of Quebec and the Parti Québécois can't do anything

without wondering how Quebecor will spin the story (interview, 2009a, June 18, translated by Colette Brin).

The executive argued further that

> there needs to be a debate in Parliament and in the National Assembly. The CRTC is washing its hands of any responsibility in the matter. There needs to be an intervention without an abuse of power....Political parties and governments need to address the issue but no one has the political courage to do so (interview, 2009a, June 18, translated by Colette Brin).

The television executive also called our attention to some changes that had occurred in Quebec since 2007 when our study was done. He noted that during 2008 and 2009, ownership groups in Quebec were pursuing "specific types of coverage," which were described as a focus on specific events, similar headlines and types of content (i.e., the same topic areas, not necessarily the same stories). As well, Quebecor appeared increasingly coherent and uniform in its overall news coverage, with the same story covered on different platforms. That political analysts (such as Luc Lavoie and Jean Lapierre) covered the same story on different platforms was seen as a potential limit to diversity. The respondent also told us that convergence was less visible in straight news coverage but more evident in opinion content and commentary. Finally, in that there are few newsrooms in Quebec, there is a clear risk that large corporations would be able to monopolize debate on important issues. Public broadcasting was seen as the stronghold of diversity in Quebec, presenting regional points of view and relying on various types of sources in news and current affairs programs (interview, 2009a, June 18, translated by Colette Brin).

A Quebec newspaper executive also told us that there were a lot of fears surrounding convergence, but that there had been significant barriers to its implementation: namely, pre-2007 collective agreements and news practices specific to each medium meant that only certain things could be shared (e.g., still images from television video). Despite these limitations, it was felt that there were intentions at Quebecor to move in the direction of content-sharing. However, Quebecor's regulatory obligation to maintain separate newsrooms played a role in blocking its convergence project. In the long run, however, content-sharing was seen as "inevitable," in that with the formation of large media groups comes development or consolidation strategies (interview, 2009, June 17, translated by Colette Brin).

The final Quebec media executive interviewed admitted that the term "convergence" had developed negative connotations, so it tended not to be used by Quebecor. Significantly, however, Quebecor's business model "is still based on convergence" (interview, 2010, Feb. 15, translated by Colette Brin). However, rather than content-sharing, selling ad space for several platforms at once (economies of scale) and having a number of profitable holdings (allowing the more profitable to subsidize the less profitable) were pointed to as chief advantages of convergence.

This media executive also reiterated an argument made in an earlier English-language interview—the need for *content exclusivity* and *differentiation*—both of which clearly work against content-sharing. He argued that "the context of news is more demanding than it was five or ten years ago. You have to allocate resources to produce a different type of coverage." As a result, newspapers "will have fewer journalists covering 'commodity news' and more working on 'exclusive news'—investigative and in-depth reporting, and follow-up stories" (interview, 2010, Feb. 15, translated by Colette Brin).

Differences between CP and QMI were discussed as well, a major one being that a very small editorial staff is assigned to QMI. Rather, the current QMI structure, which became operational in July 2010, is decentralized, composed of about 1,000 news workers across Canada (photographers, reporters and editors), mostly working in daily and weekly newspapers (Millette, 2010). The corporate strategy, according to the executive, is to use local resources rather than sending in reporters from the national media to cover events for the newspaper chain, television network and website. This reduces travel costs and also takes advantage of local perspectives and allows for long-term coverage of an issue. Greater hope for the success of QMI was seen among Quebecor's chain of English-language Sun newspapers, due to Quebec's unique labour regulations, described as "one of the places, including France and the Nordic countries, where labour parameters are most strict for the employer." While it was acknowledged that there is "a strong local culture at the *Calgary Sun* or the *London Free Press*, reporters understand that QMI, instead of being a threat, is a source of differentiation and competitive advantage" (interview, 2010, Feb. 15, translated by Colette Brin).

With respect to journalism as a profession, it was universally seen to be the case that multiple skill sets were necessary for journalists coming into the job market. It was felt, however, that multiple platform reporting would be "introduced progressively," and that there would "always be a place for specialized talent" (exceptional writers and on-air presenters). Unfortunately, cuts to newsroom staff were seen as a long-term reality rather than an accommodation to short-term financial stress: "We need to adapt to the current context, working conditions can no longer be the same as in the 1980s" (interview, 2010, Feb. 15, translated by Colette Brin).

6

Stakeholders Assess the State of Canadian Media

Background

TO COMPLETE OUR GOAL of offering a comprehensive view of the status of Canadian media in the age of cross-ownership, in 2009–2010 we also contacted politicians, policy analysts, regulators (representing the Canadian government and the Province of Quebec), Canadian journalists and labour leaders, as well as journalism professors in Canada and the United States for interviews. These interviews were less structured than those reported in the previous chapter, and while we cannot claim a critical mass of respondents in any of the above categories, nor any attempt at achieving a representative sample, we nevertheless received an interesting variety of views on a range of important and timely topics.

Views of Journalists

In April 2009, then Canwest News Service journalist David Akin wrote a three-part analysis on the status of the Canadian newspaper industry entitled "The Enduring Newspaper." In the first installment he addressed head-on the question of whether the current business model for newspapers was dead. His answer: far from it. In fact, he reported that at the end of 2008, most of Canada's 98 daily newspapers "are believed to be profitable, despite the recession," and that although 2008 saw a 5 per cent reduction in paid circulation, the combination hard copy/online audience was "the same as it was in 2003" (Akin, 2009, Apr. 25: A1). At the same time, however, he acknowledged that "Canadian and American publishers, trying to bring the costs of doing business in line with decreased revenues, have laid off staff and drastically cut costs to cope with the slowing advertising revenues" (2009, Apr. 25: A11).

Akin's optimism was derived in part from interviews with major Canadian media executives. Both *Toronto Star* publisher John Cruickshank and CEO of Canwest Publishing Dennis Skulsky argued for the viability of the Canadian newspaper industry. Cruickshank identified current problems, especially in the US, as having more to do with financing debt than with a loss of market.[1] In Cruickshank's view, "[t]here certainly will be newspapers in two years, five years, and 10 years time" (as quoted in Akin, 2009, Apr. 25: A11). Skulsky was also quite bullish on the industry, claiming that "[t]here will be newspapers....The business model in Canada, in particular, is certainly still viable, but that doesn't mean it's viable forever. We have to continue to evolve and we have to get leaner." And, in an echo of Leonard Asper's earlier emphasis on multitasking, he noted that "[w]e have to invest in the future and hire and bring people into the business that move easily among the media platforms today in a digital generation" (as quoted in Akin, 2009, Apr. 25: A11).

Akin also found optimism in the newspaper's position as a unique conveyer of advertising. According to ZenithOptimedia Canada's CEO Sunni Boot, "Newspapers work....There's immediacy to it. There's credibility to it. It's still a very, very good medium" (as quoted in Akin, 2009, Apr. 27: A8). Similarly, the *Toronto Star* publisher pointed to the unique advertising strength of newspapers:

> There still isn't an alternative to the print product that works for advertisers the way that print does....You're seeing an extraordinary fracturing (of audiences) in television and radio and you're also seeing a very rapid aging of television audiences so that we may actually get to the situation again where newspapers, by a huge margin, are the only medium that's really talking very broadly to the population. We may be the only mass medium left (Cruickshank, as quoted in Akin, 2009, Apr. 27: A8).

The final source of Akin's optimism lay in differences between the Canadian and American newspaper industries, which in combination it was argued made Canadian newspapers less vulnerable to the adverse financial conditions that took hold with a vengeance in the US beginning in the fall of 2008. In summary, these Canadian advantages were:

- a less serious decline in readership and circulation;
- a lesser dependence on classified advertising for revenue (15 per cent of overall revenues in Canada vs. 22–25 per cent in the US);
- less competition with radio for advertising business;
- a milder business recession;
- a lower cost structure;
- a greater success in integrating online applications with traditional business;
- being able to use telemarketing to recruit subscribers;
- "readership" rather than "circulation" used to calculate advertising rates;
- greater success in capturing the "insert" or "flyer" market (Akin, 2009, Apr. 29: C7).

The headline of Akin's third installment of "The Enduring Newspaper" captures the overall situation: "Canada's newspapers hold their own."

Another Canadian journalist, Terry Field, now Associate Professor of Journalism at Calgary's Mount Royal College, addressed the key question of how newspapers can make a profit on the Internet. While Field acknowledged that he never thought he would find himself "cheering for media mogul, iconoclast and right-wing rogue Rupert Murdoch," he hoped that Murdoch's plan "to make readers pay for online content [would succeed]". According to Murdoch, "Quality journalism is not cheap and the money required to do such work needs to come from somewhere." Field agreed, arguing that "the media business needs to act more boldly to create new sources of revenue." While the need for new revenue is clearly there, the question remains: "Why will someone agree to pay for something as widely available as news?" As long as there are companies offering free content (the BBC is cited as an example), "one has to wonder what would induce people to pay for content." Field pointed to another problem, that of protecting "proprietary material generated for...Internet sites from hackers who might steal it, and others who might pay for it then copy, paste and disseminate it for free." For Field, "[p]rotecting pay-per-view content will be a major hurdle for any organization" (Field, 2009, Aug. 25: A10).

A former Canadian television reporter turned academic interviewed for the study offered some professional insights into why "content-sharing has not been embraced." First he explained some of the unique attributes of TV reporting. The need for visuals largely precludes the use of telephone interviews, which implies travel. Moreover, the centrality of visual images to a story (the need to get a variety of shots, combined with visual and audio editing), which results in a story of perhaps a minute and a half (all in a culture that stresses the immediate), constitutes significant barriers to content-sharing with newspapers, which rely largely on verbal description. Attitudes of journalists in different media were also cited as important. Specifically, that "television journalists tend to see themselves as the celebrities of journalism," while print journalists regard TV as "the idiots' medium," makes each "reluctant to do the others' media." He discussed as well the "silo mentality"—that even within the same television network there is "competition between program producers, making them reluctant to share content with other programs." He argued that more than egos were involved in this mentality; ultimately budgets and the personnel they support were seen to be at stake (interview, 2009, Sept. 16).

With respect to future trends, for television news he saw greater use of the technique of reporters or anchors interviewing other reporters as "pseudo-expert sources" on a story. As well, he indicated that he would not be surprised to see newspapers adopting the use of "a TV newsroom-type set for their websites." Alternative survival strategies were presented for the CBC: "all Canadian, all the time" vs. "ratings so high that no politician could cut the budget without suffering electoral consequences." It was noted that the public broadcaster had clearly chosen the latter strategy and the wisdom of that choice was questioned. With respect to newspapers, he saw the cuts to staff as having reduced the amount of investigative work being done. Moreover, in that such work is time-consuming and expensive, it is becoming "increasingly hard to justify the 'public good' aspect of journalism" (interview, 2009, Sept. 16; further on this theme see Picard, 2007; Sonnac, 2009; Gans, 2010, and Butterworth, 2010).

As was the case with media executives we interviewed, convergence and the resultant sharing of content appeared to be of greater concern among Quebec journalists, and that concern clearly was focused on Quebecor. A Quebec-based newspaper journalist pointed out that initially, at both TVA and *Le Journal de Montréal*, there were efforts to "preserve newsroom independence"—this in the face of Pierre Karl Péladeau's purported view that "all Quebecor entities are at the service of the corporation, including journalists. He expects them to promote recording artists, films promoted or distributed by Quebecor companies, and these are in fact heavily covered in *Le Journal de Montréal* and on TVA." However, the journalist believed that in the early days of converged ownership the union could have tried harder "to make it work—to do convergence right—rather than just close the door completely. That was back in 2004–2005, during the first season of *Star Académie*. Since then, the situation has just gotten worse" (interview, 2009, June 16, translated by Colette Brin).

It was acknowledged that "convergence can be a positive thing—ideally it could be a tool to promote content diversity. If it means fewer journalists working on a story, other journalists are free to do other stories. But the reality is that they'll lose their jobs....Right now the major issues are job cuts, as well as Quebecor's vision of concentration and centralization." Centralization of control at *Le Journal de Montréal* was described as particularly problematic: "They've doubled the size of higher-level management and reduced positions at the editor level. Decisions will be made at the corporate level and there will be little or no local power, which now acts as a buffer between journalists and corporate pressure" (interview, 2009, June 16, translated by Colette Brin).

The journalist reported that at Quebecor, "there has been some journalistic convergence and corporate convergence as well." Specifically, for Quebecor, "arts and entertainment are at the heart of the convergence project, because that is where the corporate interests are." It was also reported that there had in fact been some collaboration between *Le Journal de Montréal* and TVA: "when *Journal de Montréal* does investigative work there is follow-up on TVA, and occasionally they do investigative work together. [However, because of CRTC regulations]...they do not work together." When asked if the situation had changed following the 2008 CRTC ruling that Quebecor no longer had to maintain separate newsrooms, the journalist responded that "we haven't seen the effects of that yet, only the occasional collaborative project" (interview, 2009, June 16, translated by Colette Brin).

The journalist expanded on the distinction between convergence and concentration:

Convergence is about putting all the components of the company at the service of the empire. *Concentration* means a unified perspective on information. Until now, there haven't been too many examples of concentration, but what is being asked by Quebecor would result in severe homogenization. The newspaper could contain stories from any other Quebecor entity. All barriers to protect content would be lifted. That is Pierre Karl Péladeau's vision: Why do I need five journalists to cover a story when one can do the job? (interview, 2009, June 16, translated by Colette Brin).

The financial crisis faced by Canadian newspapers was described as less severe in Quebec. "Not all newspapers are in the same financial situation. The worst off are those that were bought at a high price by companies which incurred huge debts. That isn't the case in Quebec. The *Gazette* and *Le Journal de Montréal* are profitable newspapers." *La Presse*, however, was described as "always expensive to run and not profitable. The Desmarais family was happy if it wasn't losing money" (interview, 2009, June 16, translated by Colette Brin).

The journalist believed as well that "at some point, we will have to make choices as a society to preserve some quality and diversity" and that government intervention was seen as necessary to achieve this. Such intervention, however, was not seen as likely, as there was no "political will" on the part of governments to move in that direction. It was argued that in a way, corporate concentration "makes it easier for them— fewer journalists to deal with, easier to manage. Also, media owners, especially Pierre Karl Péladeau, have developed close relationships with the government" (interview, 2009, June 16, translated by Colette Brin).

Also noted was "resistance to convergence from both [print and TV] newsrooms," with the journalist noting that "the *Journal* union has always fought to preserve newsroom independence. The union took a very harsh position on convergence very quickly, so there wasn't much room for adaptation or negotiation. However, there were some adjustments made with individual journalists." Cited as an example was the case of Richard Latendresse, a TVA foreign correspondent who also wrote a column in *Le Journal de Montréal*. This arrangement "was challenged by the union, but Quebecor argued he was hired as a specialist because of his war coverage experience." Mr. Latendresse was not, however, allowed to do general news coverage for the paper. The journalist also took note of Quebecor's move to create its own corporate news service to replace CP: "It's clear what Quebecor wants to do. They are setting up their own corporate news service to replace CP, which is also a blow to diversity" (interview, 2009, June 16, translated by Colette Brin).

Another journalist agreed that there had been only limited convergence practices at Quebecor: "My feeling is that there isn't any collusion in day-to-day reporting. It's quite rare that broadcast and print media collaborate." However, it was acknowledged that "it's obvious that Quebecor media were engaged in promoting artists and TVA variety shows. That's perhaps the most visible part of convergence." It was also felt that the lockout at Le Journal de Montréal would contribute to greater content-sharing between Quebecor print properties (interview, 2009, June 22, translated by Colette Brin).

The journalist pointed to factors other than convergence that led to similar stories: pack journalism and the fact that "journalists have very similar socioeconomic backgrounds and similar interests." With respect to pack journalism, the journalist pointed to similarities in coverage of the Quebec National Assembly:

> Sure, here and there, a reporter, a columnist will add an original perspective. But, by and large, all the stories seem remarkably similar. So there is a form of convergence because of *proximity*, rather than ownership. It's the same for reporters who cover the law courts. Working in close proximity, not wanting to get "scooped" by a competitor, or a sort of "gentleman's agreement"—all of this means that journalists covering these types of assignments tend to produce very similar work....They use the same sources, those who are willing to talk. Because you need to work fast, you go to the easiest sources—spokespersons, people you know—so you end up using the same ones (interview, 2009, June 22, translated by Colette Brin).

As well, the fact the newspapers were undergoing reductions in size meant "the news hole has gone down dramatically. So the convergence debate is kind of theoretical—there just isn't any space, so that means less use of material from outside the newsroom" (interview, 2009, June 22, translated by Colette Brin).

The journalist took the side of those who argued for content differentiation over homogenization.

> Newspapers are becoming more local. As the conventional business model becomes obsolete, you need to ask yourself how to stay current and relevant faced with Internet competition. One answer is to focus on local news, because you can offer information that is valuable to readers and isn't available on the Internet. When you have fewer pages to fill [the shrinking news hole], you focus on local news.... You offer opinion, analysis and commentary. You do special reports, investigative reporting and local news (interview, 2009, June 22, translated by Colette Brin).

This journalist agreed that newsroom cuts were counterproductive: "You're sabotaging your ability to stay current, to stay relevant....But then again, how long can you sustain losses in a business model that doesn't work?" (interview, 2009, June 22, translated by Colette Brin).

As was pointed out by a number of those we interviewed, convergence in itself did not necessarily have to be harmful:

> Some will resist convergence and use the diversity argument, but you can see it more practically. [For example,] instead of four journalists for each newspaper covering [politics in Ottawa and Quebec] you keep two and have more resources for local stories. And does the public lose? I don't think so. Of course, if it just means cutting staff without reallocating people elsewhere, that's another story (interview, 2009, June 22, translated by Colette Brin).

The final Quebec newspaper journalist interviewed agreed that arts and entertainment stories (which were not included in our study unless appearing as a news story) would likely have shown greater convergence effects, as these "are a very important source of content-sharing and cross-promotion for Quebecor." When asked whether content-sharing was a central problem in terms of news diversity, the journalist answered both "yes and no." On the one hand, "corporate news agencies and online platforms represent major changes regarding how news is produced....[For example], Gesca is renegotiating [contracts] with unions at its regional newspapers; they are looking to increase content-sharing across the chain." On the other hand, the respondent offered that the greater problem lay in the "ideological consistency of the columnists and analysts in the Quebecor media, who tend to be more right-leaning" (interview, 2010, Jan. 27, translated by Colette Brin).

The respondent noted as well that while convergence was an issue, the overall quality of Quebec journalism left much to be desired:

> It's a well-known fact that the media in general tend to cover the same news stories, and in the same way. Journalists and editors are constantly looking at what their competitor is doing and imitating each other. It's gotten worse with all-news TV networks. News is produced following the TV model, quickly, instantly, without analysis or perspective. Considering the crisis of journalism and conventional news media, it's probably the worst thing to do, there's no added value to news content. It's OK to do breaking news on the Internet, but the print newspaper should be providing more depth, giving a foundation to the news agenda (interview, 2010, Jan. 27, translated by Colette Brin).

Also critiqued was the closing of newsrooms at Télévision Quatre Saisons (TQS, renamed V in 2009, following its acquisition by Remstar) in favour of covering news through commentary-talk formats: "It's better than it was when they were doing news. The new TQS formats are done cheaply; they aren't excellent, but at least they're trying something new" (interview, 2010, Jan. 27, translated by Colette Brin).

Views of Politicians, Regulators and Policy Analysts

At the federal level a number of themes emerged from our interviews with those connected in various capacities to policy analysis and policy-making. The first, offered by a former Canadian newspaper executive with some experience in government, was that while media ownership concentration was still "a significant concern...[it is]...not the main thing we have to worry about." Singled out for that distinction was "the scary decline in newspaper readership." The latter trend was seen to be especially troubling because "the main news gatherers work in print." While the Internet was seen as offering a new model, it was noted that "strong news gathering is still needed." It was pointed out that huge buyouts and layoffs in the newspaper industry have resulted in fewer journalists, and, as a consequence, "less things get covered—trees fall in the forest with no one hearing them." In view of the decline in the number of news bureaus and a shrinking Ottawa press gallery, it was felt that "the chief need is to preserve a critical mass of reporters."

The respondent went on to offer the less than reassuring assessment that "the 20th century may have been the golden age of journalism" (interview, 2009, May 29).

On the question of the impact of concentration of media ownership, two problems were identified: the possibility of editorial direction from above (either through hiring of like-minded executives or those executives making it their business to agree with the views of ownership), and that the large debt resulting from media acquisitions at the beginning of the decade would be paid off largely by cutting news staff.

The answer to our question regarding the utility of CRTC restrictions on cross-ownership after major consolidations had already occurred was that it is "never too late" to go forward with new rules; "what is there… [in the way of media properties]…changes ownership; media pieces don't disappear—they just reconfigure" (interview, 2009, May 29), an observation confirmed by the ownership changes occurring in 2010.

Senior Canadian government policy-makers picked up on the latter point, indicating that due to the continuing concern over a plurality of voices "there had to be some clear limits, thus, further cross-ownership thresholds were established" (see CRTC, 2008-4). Respondents made the point that "the relationship between ownership and editorial voice is different in TV and newspapers," and of greater concern in the print media, which currently do not fall under government regulation (interview, 2009b, June 18).

As was the case with media executives we interviewed, the final point cited by policy-makers as a "key issue" of the future was "who controls 'the pipes'—the distribution of programming," rather than just programming content. Here it was seen as essential to maintain at least two separate distribution systems (cable and satellite) (interview, 2009b, June 18).

Kenneth Goldstein, President of Winnipeg-based Communications Management, Inc., believes firmly that "the existing business model employed by Canadian media is at the end of its useful life" (interview, 2009, Aug. 25). In printed material given to us at the interview, he argues that "[w]e are coming to the end of a 100-year-old economic model for the media industry. And that has profound implications for how, and where, we will get our news in the future" (2009: 1). Goldstein views the role of traditional media as having served as "intermediaries, connecting content, consumers and advertisers." Technology, opening the door to citizen-producers of content, has challenged this role by enabling those producers "to send media-like content directly to consumers" (2009: 1). The result: "*For the first time in history, on a mass scale, the means of production and distribution for information and entertainment products are finding their way into the hands of consumers*" (2009: 2, italics in the original).

This new reality offers a profound challenge to conventional media, which depend on the majority of their revenues from advertisers, not the mass public, the ultimate consumers of their product. Citing the relationship between how journalism is practiced and how it is paid for (the true cost of content always having been far greater than the price paid directly for it by consumers), for Goldstein, "these changes...[move us]... closer to an uncertain future" (2009: 6). The trend in television has been toward more specialty channels, which, through within-company "repurposing of profits," could help carry the less profitable conventional channels. The financial problem for newspapers is compounded by the fact that much Internet content (including that of some major newspapers) is free, and "as long as reasonable substitutes are free, charging for content will be difficult." In terms of the future, Goldstein sees hope for a stable circulation base for paid dailies at somewhere between 30 and 35 per cent of households, an even more "intensely local" focus than is currently the case, and "a further contraction in the number of daily newspapers in Canada." He notes that he did not make the final prediction "lightly or with any pleasure....The idealized notion of alternative competing voices is a good thing. But it is precisely because of the number of alternative competing voices, and consumer acceptance of those voices, that traditional media are shrinking" (2009: 13–14).

In a personal interview Goldstein elaborated on some of his views as well as responding to some specific questions. Specifically, we asked him if he was surprised at our findings showing a lack of shared content. He indicated that he was not surprised, noting that "the structure was wrong to encourage such sharing." We then asked him if the Canwest News Service and Quebecor's QMI offered such a structure and he believed that they did. When asked about the impact of these new commercial news services on CP, he foresaw a period where a number of news services would be competing in the marketplace (interview, 2009, Aug. 25).

Government regulators from Quebec were of the opinion that there was a high level of similarity in news content across all media, independent of ownership convergence, and that greater similarity would be found in television/television story pairs (representing different ownership groups) than in television/newspaper story pairs (from the same ownership group). However, specifically with respect to convergence, in a joint interview with regulators it was acknowledged that "it seems clear that Quebecor has been holding back until now, but it's likely that there will be an increase of content-sharing within Quebecor-owned media. The creation of the QMI news agency and the attempted centralization of National Assembly coverage testify to these intentions." It was also noted that Radio-Canada was "restructuring its news operation to favour multiplatform reporting and collaboration between TV, radio and the Internet." All of this said, the general view was that convergence "did not seem to be a major cause for concern"—more problematic were "shrinking resources across media companies, lack of in-depth coverage and the growing gap between 'elite' and 'ordinary' news sources," whereby paid content would be consumed by an elite audience prepared to pay for premium information, while the general public would consume free, lower-quality news (interview, 2009, Sept. 24, translated by Colette Brin).

It was pointed out that the provincial government had blogging and citizen journalism on its radar, wanting to offer "accreditation to ethical blogs" in exchange for a fee. While an ethical responsibility to ensure "moderation" in website material was acknowledged, limited resources were cited as the reason for not moving forward. Interestingly, the Quebec Press Council did not have a specific "convergence file" but would consider opening one if journalistic quality becomes a concern (interview, 2009, Sept. 24, translated by Colette Brin).

When asked if we would have found more shared content if the study had been done two years later, the answer was "yes," as "the economic crisis has accelerated the trend toward content-sharing." It was noted, however, that in view of labour conflicts (Le Journal de Montréal), negotiations (La Presse, TVA) and major restructuring of newsrooms (Radio-Canada)—"all media are affected, not only cross-owned television and newspaper [operations]. How this all will take shape in the Quebec media landscape will appear more clearly once the current conflict and restructuring efforts have ended or at least stabilized." In short, media convergence in Quebec "is still very much a moving target" (interview, 2009, Sept. 24, translated by Colette Brin).

A second participant in the interview offered that "the professional culture of journalism" was changing in that there were "increasing limits to journalistic autonomy" in the form of stricter managerial controls on news production and editorial directives. Further, the pursuit of original coverage to establish "a strong news brand," which requires resources that only larger companies can afford, is an argument offered in favour of consolidation. It was pointed out that there was "widespread concern in the province about the influence of large media companies," but not particularly on content-sharing, which was seen as "too specific—the public doesn't see it." Nevertheless, the current economic crisis was seen as "accelerating the trend toward content-sharing." The most popular solution to date has been "to cut back on newsroom staff and 'clone' material on different platforms." Finally, it was acknowledged that changes in Quebec media industries would appear in the next few years. These changes, whatever they might be, were described as "likely to be profound" (interview, 2009, Sept. 24, translated by Colette Brin).

Another Quebec media regulator was likewise not overly concerned with content-sharing: "[M]y general impression is that cross-ownership has no impact on editorial content. I'd say it isn't a cause for concern, except for journalists and academics." However, the respondent "expected [to see] more convergence" than was found in our study, especially between *Le Journal de Montréal* and TVA. Agreement was expressed that "the lockout at *Le Journal de Montréal* will certainly increase convergence....It's tempting for a newspaper owner to share content across publications. The content may be trashy, but it works." As with everyone we interviewed in Quebec, it was felt that arts and entertainment were likely to be most subject to content-sharing (interview, 2009, Oct. 1, translated by Colette Brin).

The major concern expressed by the regulator was not with television news but with newspapers: "I think we need to be concerned more about newspapers, whether they can survive, and whether ownership concentration (including cross-ownership) is a problem." Such problems were seen to be greater in Quebec, where there is less diversity in local news "because there is less money due to a smaller advertising market" (interview, 2009, Oct. 1, translated by Colette Brin).

As was pointed out by others, the introduction of convergence practices to journalism in Quebec was seen as particularly difficult. "Joint news gathering makes sense as a way of optimizing resources. There is no objection to this in English Canada, including unions, only in Quebec. Here there is an aversion to risk, a precautionary principle which isn't necessarily a good thing for journalism" (interview, 2009, Oct. 1, translated by Colette Brin).

The Senate Committee's *Final Report on the Canadian News Media* dealt in-depth with the question of the future of news-gathering, pointing out that "about one-third to one-half of news and editorial content found in Canadian newspapers comes from news agencies, wire services or press associations," the main one, of course, being The Canadian Press. Citing the possible appearance of rival, for-profit news services, the committee expressed concern "that the economic viability of CP may be under threat," which it pointed out "could have consequences on the universal accessibility of a diversity of news and information in Canada." The report went on: "If CP or comparable wire services no longer existed, small, independent news organizations would be less able to cover international, national and, at times, even regional stories. This would be detrimental to the existing diversity of news voices in Canada." The report urged "subscriber shareholders to continue support for Canada's only national news service, Canadian Press" (Canada, 2006). This exhortation appears to have been overtaken by events, and, as noted, the future of CP was a concern for many to whom we spoke, but only in Quebec was government intervention mentioned as possibly needed (interview, 2009, June 16; interview, 2009a, June 18, both translated by Colette Brin).[2]

Views of Journalism Educators

American journalism professor John Merrill picked up on the consequences of some of Ken Goldstein's observations—namely a trend toward the emergence of "citizen journalists," which he saw as leading to the deprofessionalization of journalism, at least as a short-term outcome. This development was not looked upon favourably by Merrill, who expressed hope that in time journalism would regain its credentials as a professional occupation (e-mail correspondence, 2009, June 23). This view was also expressed by the publisher of a leading Canadian daily newspaper. Specifically, that "citizen journalism is not the answer...reporters need skills," especially with respect to "finding sources and providing interpretation" (interview, 2009, Sept. 1).

On a more practical level, with respect to how journalism is being taught in Canada, Professor Alan Bass of Thompson Rivers University told us "there is no question anymore that journalists of the future will be expected to be capable of reporting and telling stories in any and all formats." Moreover, he believes that "J-schools in Canada are adjusting curricula to prepare their graduates for this new workplace reality" (e-mail correspondence, 2009, Aug. 26). And, on the industry side, in response to a question regarding multitasking, an editor of a major Canadian daily newspaper reported hiring at least one new reporter on the basis of a skill in photography and "comfort in standing in front of a video camera" for the newspaper's online newscasts. The editor added, however, that "skill in story-telling" remained the highest priority in hiring (interview, 2009, Aug. 24). Another newspaper editor agreed: "the expectation is that you have multi-skill sets" (interview, 2009, Aug. 26). A newspaper publisher added his view that while "journalism is not a growth area;...those who are hired will have multiple skills" (interview, 2009, Sept. 1). A former journalist believed that the industry has in fact overreacted in terms of staff reductions, "cutting fat, muscle, and bone," and that there is a future for multiskilled journalists (interview, 2009, Sept. 16).[3]

Views of Labour

Lise Lareau, President of the Canadian Media Guild, joined others in not identifying cross-ownership-inspired content-sharing as the chief problem confronting Canadian media; accorded pride of place was the "decline of content," as she pointed out that "thousands of jobs have been lost over the past twenty years." As a result of "the drain of people... all media do pretty much the same top-five stories, often with the benefit of CP content." She noted that "with seasoned editors going out the door, what is missing is the capacity to do the next tier of stories...and complex stories are not getting covered." She noted that in journalism, "experience matters and has a price, ...[but that currently]...media is a tough business if you're in your fifties." She saw the industry as "as in the middle of a transition," with the end point "hard to see." However, the "period of layoffs" was not seen as having ended (interview, 2009, Sept. 3).

Lareau observed that "in a period of rapid change, people fear for survival...[and as a consequence]...make bad decisions." She was especially concerned with the implications of corporate news services on news content, in that she described CP as "setting the news agenda for the first tier of stories." She was not surprised at Canwest's decision to turn to its own news service in that the company had always taken a "hard-line" on content profits. However, in the upcoming competition among rival news services, she believed that CP would emerge as "the last true information provider standing" (interview, 2009, Sept. 3).[4]

She also offered a number of views regarding journalists' workloads and where the industry was headed with respect to multitasking. She described "the pressure to do more with less...[as]...intense," with the expectation being that journalists will "serve all three media lines... [print, television and Internet, noting that currently] at CP people do it all." In fact, workload was cited as "the big issue [in contract negotiations] of this era—bigger than compensation—with employers pushing to get more with less." The implication of this is that journalists coming on stream will need "the skills to be able to communicate on-camera and in writing." She pointed out as well that styles of writing for the Internet, as well as the type of stories, differ from those of traditional writing for print. "Writing for the eye on computer screens" requires shorter sentences, while there is far greater need on the Internet for "backgrounders, colour pieces, supplementary insight pieces, and archival material." She noted that currently the CBC had different reporters providing content for their website. As was the case with the newspaper editors we interviewed, Lareau believed that journalists of the future "will have to be able to do on-camera [work]" (interview, 2009, Sept. 3).

7

Old Media, New Media, Any Media?

The Content Analysis

BASED ON A COMPARISON OF TV and newspaper story pairs from both cross-owned and separately owned media, our research has provided us with a first-time snapshot of the degree to which newly converged Canadian national media organizations, in both official languages, subsequently engaged in the practice of content-sharing. Flagship newspapers and prime-time television news programs from CTVglobemedia, Canwest Global Communications and Quebecor were paired for four weeks in 2007 to examine the similarity of information within stories dealing with the same subject. Newspaper and television groups not linked by ownership were also studied as a control to ensure that any similarities found could in fact be attributed to ownership and were not due to the nature of news events themselves and/or to other factors. Canwest local-market television and newspaper platforms in Edmonton, Alberta, were studied as well for similarities in story content to assess whether local markets proved to be more susceptible or amenable to content-sharing.

The results of our paired comparison of television and newspaper stories failed to confirm the hypothesis that informational convergence had occurred in any of our cross-owned test groups. While some story dimensions yielded statistically significant results, in some of these cases the greater content similarity was seen unexpectedly among the control groups. Overall, well under 10 per cent of story pairs in all categories of ownership studied fell into the "very similar" category on our national media index scale. In any event, on close examination of all "very similar" story pairs, we were able to document that only one story had in fact been shared in virtual identical form, in this case between Edmonton Global's *News Hour* and the *Edmonton Journal*, indirectly by way of The Canadian Press. In fact, most similarities in story content were traced to the use of wire services, chiefly CP press releases or press conferences/scrums. While our expectations (or fears) about content-sharing were not confirmed, our findings stand as a benchmark for a time when media convergence was in its infancy in Canada.[1]

Explaining the Lack of Content-Sharing

What accounts for the lack of evidence to support critics' claims that there would be less diversity in news as a result of cross-ownership? For this we must look first to the American research on converged newsrooms reviewed in chapter 2. Even in the United States, where a limited number of converged newsrooms had been created, researchers failed to document content-sharing, much less full convergence, being practiced (see Huang et al., 2004; Quandt and Singer, 2009). While media owners such as Leonard Asper may have dreamt of journalists being able to work in different platforms (2001), there appeared to be considerable reluctance on the part of journalists themselves to accommodate this dream; this was especially the case in Quebec, where resistance was fierce. There were as well significant structural constraints imposed by the differing journalistic styles of the two media involved, and in Quebec there was a regulatory separation of newsrooms at Quebecor, as well as restrictive pre-2007 union contracts.

It is, of course, possible that the lack of shared content between components of "old media" could reflect a conscious decision on the part of owners and managers *not to converge* these media in terms of content-sharing. In fact, we found in our interviews that while Canwest media platforms were encouraged to work together, "no specific direction" was offered with respect to sharing of content (interview, 2009, Aug. 27).

Contrariwise, it was felt that Quebecor would have pressed harder for convergence had not it been for the CRTC restrictions (interview, 2009,

June 6). At any rate, the push toward convergence appears to be largely the result of changes in digital technology and the realization that the audiences and readership for "old media" were being challenged by the "new media," linked to the Internet and other mechanisms for obtaining content. Thus, it may be unreasonable to expect that newspapers would try to encroach on television, or that television reporters would start writing for newspapers, given that the two types of journalism are so different. Rather, digital convergence suggests that both newspapers and television will try to attract and retain audiences by providing at least some of their existing content using new delivery mechanisms—chiefly their websites. As at this point the second iteration of convergence beginning in 2010 (vertical integration) appears to involve securing access to entertainment content rather than reorganizing journalistic practice (see Postscript, this volume), this is where, at least in the short term, we believe the future of convergence in Canadian journalism lies.[2]

The lack of content convergence found in the present study no doubt reflects the tension between the traditional boundaries of journalism and new demands, as the skills involved in writing for print are so different from broadcast journalism that reporters' own sense of what is "good journalism" is compromised when they cross over to an alternative medium.[3]

Finally, it is important to stress that the lack of similarity among the story elements investigated in our content analysis study does not address questions regarding the *quality* of content or whether the information available in Canada's mass media is limited in its variety, especially with respect to providing alternative viewpoints to mainstream perspectives. Nor does the study deal with the question of those issues that were not covered by major media outlets, although a convincing case might be made for their newsworthiness.[4] An examination of these questions would have required a very different research approach than the one employed in this study.

Content-sharing between newspaper and television platforms of cross-owned media companies clearly has not happened in Canada, and while there is likely to be somewhat more content-sharing in the future resulting from the turn to corporate news services (with the exception perhaps of Quebecor's QMI), this did not appear to our interviewees to constitute a major problem. In fact, two of our interviewees argued that *content differentiation* between media platforms was the preferred corporate strategy over *content-sharing*. Nevertheless, the move toward corporate news services as replacements to CP created a new set of problems that we shall touch upon below.

With respect to our finding that content-sharing had not occurred, it appears that there are basically two ways of achieving cost savings—those focused "within media properties" and those focused "across media properties." The rapid move to cross-ownership at the beginning of the new century led to widely held expectations that the focus of the new cross-media owners would be on "across media" attempts to achieve cost-saving synergies. At least in the short term, our data show that this has not worked, as far as we can determine, mainly because of structural problems involved in two very different types of media and a realization on the part of management that there were in fact limited gains to be made, given the very different styles of journalism and competencies of the journalists involved. Instead, to deal with current financial difficulties, media organizations engaged in major cost-cutting *within* each media type (mainly through reductions in staff and closing or consolidation of news bureaus), strategies that many feel have been disastrous to the quality of information in Canadian media, and it is likely that they have not yet fully run their course.

The Future of Canadian Media

Regarding the future of Canadian mass media, current business models for both conventional television and newspapers have been described as "under stress" (if not "broken") as a result of audience fragmentation and loss of advertising revenues. As mentioned, the "crisis," as it has been called by some, has been addressed mainly by "within media retrenchment"—a reduction in TV and newspaper staff through buyouts and layoffs, as well as some actual closures (e.g., Transcontinental's Halifax *Daily News* and CTV's CKX-TV) and threats of other closures (e.g., Gesca's *La Presse*, Canwest's CHEK-TV and CTV's "A Channels") (Kimber, 2008, Feb. 24; Krachinsky, 2009, Oct. 3; Marotte, 2009, Sept. 4: B3; *Financial Post*, 2009, Sept. 5; CP, 2009, Mar. 2). Indeed, the sheer reduction in the number of journalists covering key events has been cited by a number of those we interviewed as the most serious problem facing Canadian mass media.

For conventional commercial television channels, a possible survival strategy suggested involves redirecting profits from financially healthy specialty channels, combined with a strong local news focus for local stations. Others have pointed to vertical integration (combining "carriage and content") in cable and satellite companies, such as exist within Quebecor and occurred in the US with Comcast's purchase of NBC, and with BCE's recent purchase of CTV. For the CBC the situation is less clear, as these options do not appear available. The public broadcaster appears to be left with finding greater financial support from the government or increasing its commercial advertising revenues through building a greater audience share. In that the former has been tried repeatedly without success, out of necessity, it appears to have chosen to focus its efforts on the second option (interview with Lareau, 2009, Sept. 3; Dixon and Bradshaw, 2009, Oct. 31).[5]

In Quebec it was suggested that cross-promotion and content-sharing were being practiced at Radio-Canada. As well, the Radio-Canada partnership with Gesca newspapers, especially *La Presse*, was raised as a concern in interviews. More recently, the integration of radio and TV newsrooms in Montreal has caused radio journalists to fear a loss of "identity" (Cyberpresse.ca, 2010, May 21). Radio-Canada was also described somewhat differently as not involved in convergence per se, but rather in developing "specialized multiplatform units" (such as business news and investigative reporting) to leverage expertise to increase depth of coverage. This process started in 2006 with coverage of Afghanistan and involved a centralized assignment desk and specialty areas. Radio-Canada has also taken steps to integrate radio, TV and web applications, as well as experimenting with different formats and social media.

In terms of the future, it was argued that people still get their news mostly from television and that it is important not to throw out the baby with the bathwater. A Quebec television executive made the point that "if we don't want to lose people under 35, we need the same quality content on all platforms....We need to examine how we can offer a strong news brand—a focus on depth and credibility—our specific strengths....The evening newscast still has an important role—the last word of the day" (interview, 2009a, June 18, translated by Colette Brin).

For newspapers, the future appears open to a number of possible scenarios. No one with whom we spoke subscribed to the worst-case scenario—the "disappearance" of the newspaper as a print product. In fact, most adopted the mid-range position—that the newspaper will survive, perhaps in smaller numbers than exist now, with those surviving being less profitable, smaller in size and staff, and having a reduced core readership.

However, we also found a more optimistic view. Traditionally, newspapers have competed with newspapers, and television stations have competed with television stations. New technology has changed this, as now both compete for an audience on the Internet, including, interestingly, television and newspaper properties owned by the same corporation in the same market. And, given the advantages in size of news-gathering staff enjoyed by newspapers, it is by no means clear which medium will win out in dominating news production for the web, which appears to focus largely on breaking news. Paradoxically, the Internet, which many have seen as leading to the demise of the newspaper, is seen by some (but certainly not all) as its ultimate salvation. The key to the success of both the second and third scenarios is, of course, contingent on finding ways to make online content profitable.

Journalism Education

The message that we received from virtually everyone to whom we spoke was that in the journalism of the future, multitasking would be the "new normal," with all the implications this entails for current journalism school curricula. Our sense is that the country's journalism schools are at the beginning stages of a rethinking of their educational priorities. "Citizen journalism" was not seen as a viable alternative to professional journalism, based both on the need for knowledge regarding key sources to consult for a story and background information needed to give context to a news event and interpret it in a meaningful way for audiences. And, while there will be fewer paying jobs in mass media, those that become available will go to journalists with multiple or highly specialized skills.

Final Thoughts

It was widely felt that the turn to the corporate news service model initiated by Canwest in 2007 (and followed by Quebecor) would in fact serve as a vehicle for achieving greater "across-media" content-sharing synergies. How effective this strategy will be is an open question, especially for Canwest properties, which, following a filing for bankruptcy protection in early October 2009, did not survive as a "converged company" (Robertson and Willis, 2009, Oct. 7; Willis, 2009, Oct. 8). In any event, the implication of the corporate news service model for future researchers is that a study similar to the one reported here should be done in five years' time to see how much content-sharing actually will have been achieved by Quebecor under the corporate model.

There appears to be a more serious fallout from the switch to the corporate news service model, in that it creates a huge challenge for the cooperative CP wire service as a viable institution. If CP fails or is significantly marginalized under the new proposed ownership structure, what will be lost? It has been pointed out that neither the former Canwest nor Quebecor holdings, either individually or together, stretch across all of Canada, leaving significant parts of the country uncovered. This would suggest the loss of a "national voice." For example, Lise Lareau has pointed out CP's critical role in defining the first-tier stories of the day. And what of international reporting, where CP has been the dominant source of international news for Canadian papers (Sutcliffe et al., 2009)?

Finally, what about diversity? The 2006 *Final Report* of the Senate Committee implies a *loss of diversity* in media content should CP founder. On the other hand, it can be argued that in fact CP has been the great "homogenizer" in Canadian journalism, and that competing corporate news services would most likely *increase* content diversity. This question refocuses our attention on the discussion in chapter 1 regarding how much diversity is actually beneficial in a country as diverse as Canada. In that CP has functioned as a "network," with media outlets throughout the country adding content as well as drawing it from the wire, it can be seen as having set a much needed *national agenda* that arguably will be missed. Will a new concern among critics be that there is too much diversity in content to maintain a sense of political community at the national level?

It has been said that in the contemporary world, "change is the only constant," and there is perhaps no sector of society where change is more prominent than in the media, whether that change be in ownership, technology, personnel or business models. In fact, all are in play, all of the time, as the recent changes in ownership at Canwest and CTVglobemedia television and newspaper properties readily attest.

We have studied one such important change that began about a decade ago—*ownership convergence*—and concluded that in the short run at least, the worst fears associated with that particular change have not come to pass. While not completely absent in English Canada, fears regarding the impact of cross-ownership on democratic practice were greatest in Quebec and mainly focused on Quebecor, which interestingly is the only one of our companies left standing in its 2007 configuration. As well, it was suggested by at least one respondent that "the grand dream of convergence was perhaps ten years too early," while another told us that we had conducted our study "too soon to expect to see results." A Quebec media regulator commented that "convergence is still very much a moving target," an observation with which we fully concur.

Be this as it may, the fact that we did not find widespread content-sharing should not promote a sense of complacency, as new problems and concerns (many identified by those we interviewed and reported in the previous two chapters) have arisen to challenge media owners, executives and journalists, government policy-makers and regulators, journalism educators and ordinary citizens alike. We fully realize that at the end of this project we have left students and researchers an impressive agenda of unanswered questions to be addressed, and we believe that this is as it should be.

Postscript

THERE ARE OBVIOUS RISKS involved in any academic study of mass media ownership in Canada—namely huge volatility; as Christopher Waddell (2009) has noted, today's success stories might well turn out to be tomorrow's bankruptcies and vice versa. There is no doubt that the media ownership landscape in Canada changed dramatically since our study began in 2007, and, as this book was nearing completion, a number of key developments occurred in all three media companies we studied that we felt needed to be addressed in more than footnote fashion as they brought into play a new set of issues to engage both policy-makers and scholars.

Canwest Global

The first of these developments is that the Asper family no longer controls Canwest Global Communications and that their TV and newspaper properties now continue on under new and separate ownership. On October 6, 2009, after years of struggling to service a near $4-billion debt, a significant portion of which was incurred to buy Conrad Black's Hollinger newspaper chain in 2000 (Robertson, 2009, Nov.), Canwest's television holdings, plus the *National Post*, were granted protection from their creditors pending a corporate restructuring that was widely expected to see the Asper family lose control of the company (Willis, 2009, Oct. 2; Robertson and Willis, 2009, Oct. 7; Pitts, 2009, Oct. 7; Willis, 2009, Oct. 8).

Early on in the bankruptcy proceedings, the *National Post* was shifted to the company's newspaper group "to align the company's chain of papers under one subsidiary" (Robertson, 2009, Oct. 30: B1). Following this realignment, in January 2010 the newspaper arm of Canwest joined its television properties in filing for bankruptcy protection (Austen, 2010, Jan. 10).

By early May 2010, both sets of assets tentatively had been sold—the television properties to cable provider Shaw Communications (pending CRTC approval), and the full chain of newspapers to a consortium of investors headed by *National Post* publisher Paul Godfrey (see Flavelle and Spears, 2010, Feb. 12; Robertson and Krashinsky, 2010, May 11). At the beginning of July 2010, the successor newspaper company announced its new name—"Postmedia Network Canada Corp." (Sturgeon, 2010, July 2). The impact of the breakup of Canwest's television and newspaper properties signalled the end of ownership convergence at Canwest and would most likely end any future plans for content-sharing between what are now two separate successor companies.

More importantly, however, the Canwest breakup was but the "first shoe to drop" in what has turned out to be the end of the "first age of media convergence" in Canada and marked the beginning of the second. In a preview of possible future concerns, in early December 2009, US cable provider Comcast purchased "a majority interest in NBC Universal for $13.75 billion." The deal gave "the nation's largest cable TV provider" control over "the...[NBC]...network, an array of cable channels and a major movie studio." It was noted that as a result of the purchase, Comcast would control both production and distribution, and this raised *"concern that Comcast will wield too much power in the entertainment industry"* (msnbc, 2009, Dec. 3, italics added). We can speculate that similar concerns will be voiced over Shaw Communications' purchase of Canwest Global's television properties and the September 2010 BCE purchase of the CTV network, which ended the attempt at horizontal convergence of newspapers and television as configured in CTVglobemedia. Of course, it should be noted that Quebecor has had all the pieces in place for a vertical integration model consisting of both "pipes" and content for some time. The recent launch of Vidéotron's wireless network may in fact signal a new convergence strategy focused on mobile devices (Marlow, 2010, Sept. 9). In any event, BCE's acquisition of CTV leaves Telus as the only major Canadian telecom company that is without its own in-house supply of content (Marlow, 2010, Sept. 11).

ctvglobemedia

As Head of BCE, Jean Monty championed the 2000 convergence strategy leading to the creation of Bell Globemedia, and was identified by Gordon Pitts (2002) as one of the five "Kings of Convergence." Monty was forced to resign his position in 2002, and his successor, Michael Sabia, was suspicious of convergence. In 2005, Sabia reduced BCE's ownership stake in Bell Globemedia in favour of the Thomson family.

In June 2006, shortly after gaining control of Bell Globemedia, Kenneth Thomson died. His son David had assumed control of the company in 2002, and in 2007, had negotiated the purchase of rival content producer Reuters (Olive, 2007, May 5). More to our area of interest, minority owner BCE began negotiating the complete sale of itself to a private consortium. This sale was challenged in the courts and was only given final approval in the summer of 2008. In the fall of 2009, the whole deal fell through, an apparent victim of the meltdowns of financial markets that signalled the beginning of the "Great Recession."

In early September 2010, in a complete reversal of its 2005 significant ownership divestment from ctvglobemedia, BCE, Canada's largest telecommunications company, under new leadership, announced that pending CRTC approval, it would acquire "ownership of the CTV Network, TSN and a clutch of specialty channels" (but not the *Globe and Mail*) for $1.3 billion. According to BCE President George Cope, BCE's goal is to become "the largest provider of TV in Canada" by 2015 (as quoted in Marlow, 2010, Sept. 11: B1). And, as explained by Ian Marlow, "[a]s TV and video content spreads rapidly from TV's to laptops and onto smartphones, Bell may be in position to make that possible—a feat that would have been laughable a few years earlier" (2010, Sept. 11: B1).

According to Gordon Pitts, "Clearly this is Convergence 2.0, another round in the vision of combining media content and delivery over multiple channels, and astonishingly, BCE is a player again." The BCE president, however, chose not to use the word "convergence" to describe the new venture; rather he called it "the 'triple play' of putting the Internet, telecommunications and television together into one powerful entity." Pitts explains what changed from the time of the 2000 "convergence orgy [that] became a graveyard of executive dreams at places such as AOL Time Warner, Canwest Global, and to some extent BCE and Quebecor Inc.: ...[t]he dollars being spent are clearly more restrained now, the strategy less grandiose. Also the technological potential is now a reality, in the capacity to deliver vast bandwidth in video images over wireless networks" (Pitts, 2010, Sept. 10: B4). Ian Marlow summarizes the changes at BCE:

> Before [the CTV acquisition], Bell was a part of the old telecom regime: A simple set of pipes, a pure distributor of satellite and Internet-based TV products, Internet, home phone and wireless. Now, with CTV, Bell is now an equal with Quebecor and Shaw as the distributors negotiate for the lucrative rights to show each other's content (2010, Sept. 11: B6).

As a result of the BCE purchase of CTV, two major Canadian newspapers, the *Globe and Mail* (now owned by the Thomson family) and the *Toronto Star* (still owned by Torstar) are no longer linked in ownership with electronic media (Krashinsky, 2010, Sept. 11: B8).

Quebecor

Finally, it must be pointed out that all the research for this book was conducted well before the announcement of Quebecor's intent to enter the English TV news market with its bid to start a SUN-TV all-news channel "to be modeled on ratings-rich Fox News in the United States" (Chase, 2010, June 11: A7).

Quebecor's SunTVNews, an all-news network launched during the federal election campaign on April 18, 2011, was mired in controversy.[1] When it was first announced in March 2010, detractors labelled it "Fox News North," referring to the provocative tone and conservative slant of the US network. Some have also alleged possible interference in the CRTC licensing process on the basis of Quebecor's close ties with the Conservative Government (see Martin, 2010, Aug. 19). Kory Teneycke, a former spokesman for Prime Minister Stephen Harper, had been hired initially to head the project. Teneycke stepped down during the CRTC licensing process and returned to Sun News in January 2011. An online petition asking the CRTC to block funding of the new channel from cable fees was circulated by the international activist group Avaaz.org. Quebecor revised its licence application to the CRTC, backing down on its request for "must-offer" status (Krashinsky, 2010, Oct. 5).

In light of Quebecor's decision to pull out of both the Quebec and Alberta Press Councils, described by retired Justice and Quebec Press Council President John Gomery as "unthinkable" (as quoted in Martini, 2010, July 6), the question that undoubtedly will be asked in the coming years is whether the greater political polarization likely to be generated by a dedicated "conservative" English-language news channel will be beneficial for Canadian democracy. We anticipate a spirited debate on this issue.

On the labour front, the *Journal de Montréal* union and Quebecor management reached an agreement in February 2011, after a lockout that lasted just over two years. Although Quebecor offered to provide jobs for only 62 of the 200 locked-out workers (including 42 in the newsroom), in early April only 23 journalists had agreed to return to the newspaper (Cameron, 2011, Apr. 4). *Rue Frontenac*, the news website and weekly newspaper created by the locked-out workers, continues to be published but it is unclear as of this writing how many journalists it will be able to support (during the conflict, journalists were paid through the union's strike fund). In an interview given after the dispute had been resolved, Quebecor CEO Pierre Karl Péladeau blamed the labour federation Confédération des syndicats nationaux (CSN) for failing to take into account the recent evolution of the newspaper industry in its negotiation strategy. He added that consolidation of operations, including newsrooms, was inevitable in the current context (Desplanques, 2011, Apr. 5).

Notes

1 Media and Democratic Governance

1. At the time of the Vidéotron acquisition, Quebecor already owned the Télévision Quatre Saisons (TQS) network. In that the acquisition of TVA involved a major newspaper chain purchasing a major television network, the CTRC forced Quebecor to give up its ownership of TQS as a condition of acquiring TVA. As well, Quebecor voluntarily offered to keep the editorial functions of its newspapers and newly acquired television properties separate, a condition rescinded by the CRTC in 2008 (see CRTC, 2008-5).
2. In December 2006, Bell Globemedia announced a change in name to CTVglobemedia effective January 1, 2007. The name change was made to reflect BCE's reduced share of the company from 68.5 per cent to 15 per cent. Other stakeholders in CTVglobemedia were reported to be the Woodbridge Company Ltd. (representing the Thomson family) holding 40 per cent, Ontario Teacher's Pension Plan holding 25 per cent, and Torstar Corporation holding 20 per cent (BCE, 2006).
3. It should be pointed out that Power Corporation (Gesca) also owns all of the French-language regional dailies in Quebec, excluding Quebecor's *Journal de Québec*, and controls roughly half of the daily newspaper circulation in the province. We are not implying that Gesca newspapers are in fact "independent," just that they are not linked in ownership with television properties.
4. Interestingly, the national editorials did not run in the corporation's flagship newspaper, the *National Post*.
5. A more complete review of scholarly literature dealing with convergence follows in chapter 2.
6. Although the ambitious task of "nation-building" is now seen to be beyond even the mandate of the public broadcaster, if the contentious

issues associated with these societal cleavages are to be resolved within a framework that is seen to be reasonably equitable, following democratic theory, at minimum the positions associated with these divides need to have access to the country's mass media (see Fleras, 2001).

7. Another major argument offered by media owners in favour of convergence is the ability to offer advertisers a variety of platforms at a discounted price.

8. Indeed, Canwest Global's 2007 decision to leave the Canadian Press cooperative news service in favour of creating its own Canwest News Service, followed by the announcement by Quebecor that it would be doing the same in 2010, indicates that this has already happened. We will discuss the implications of these decisions in the concluding chapter.

9. As far as we can determine, Torstar's involvement in CTVglobemedia was entered into as an *investment strategy*, rather than as a prelude to an *active management role*. At the moment of this writing at least, this strategy does not appear to have changed. Torstar has since sold its investment in CTV.

10. Studies by Statistics Canada suggest that following an initial surge between 1997 and 2001, use of the Internet has stabilized, leaving it as a secondary news source (Statistics Canada, 2003). Data reported by the Canadian Media Research Consortium in 2004 showed the Internet was used as a news source by 17.1 per cent of Canadians daily, placing it far behind national and local television (viewed by 53.5 per cent and 54.9 per cent, respectively daily), radio (listened to by 56.5 per cent daily) and equal to local newspapers (read by 17.1 per cent daily). Use of the Internet was very close to the 18.9 per cent of Canadians reporting reading a national newspaper daily. Significant for the issue of content diversity, according to the Canadian Media Research Consortium (CMRC) study, the most frequently used websites for news are those controlled by large media organizations (msn.com, cbc.ca, yahoo.com, theglobeandmail.ca and canada.com [Canadian Media Research Consortium, 2004]). In short, the content on "mainstream Internet" sites is very likely to closely mirror that appearing on the pages of parent-company newspapers and on the newscasts of their television networks (for similar conclusions in the UK, see Luft, 2008).

A 2007 study by the Canadian Internet Project (CIP-RIC) "showed online activities appear to supplement rather than displace traditional media use." Professor Charles Zamaria of Ryerson University challenged the conventional wisdom that "would suggest that Internet use has increased at the expense of traditional media." According to Zamaria, "'the amount of time spent attending to conventional media by Internet users and non-users is virtually identical. In general, we found that Internet users are not finding time to be online by taking away from their traditional media diet. In many ways, media activity just begets more media activity'" (as quoted in CIP-RIC, 2008, Sept. 24). A 2010 study by Centre d'études sur les médias indicates that in Quebec at least, news consumption remains dominated by conventional mass media (84 per cent of total news consumption time), but that the Internet is growing (16 per cent, compared to 12.7 per cent in 2007). According to Statistics Canada's (2010) Canadian Internet Use Study, 80 per cent of Canadians use the Internet, and among this group, 68 per cent access "news and sports" online. Especially among younger Canadians the Internet is obviously a growth area and any assessments regarding its use are very likely to reflect increased use.

2 Convergence: Promises and Problems

1. In 2007, the Federal Communications Commission in the United States voted "to modestly relax its existing ban on newspaper/broadcast cross-ownership, which had been in effect for more than 30 years." Under the old rule, cross-ownership of newspaper/broadcast properties in the same market had been banned. Under the new rules, proposals for cross-ownership would be reviewed "*on a case-by-case basis to determine whether it would be in the public interest—specifically, whether it would promote competition, localism, and diversity.*" The guidelines are based on market size, with tighter restrictions applied to smaller markets where cross-ownership is presumed to be "not in the public interest." Regardless of market size, all proposed combinations also will be reviewed in terms of four factors: the extent to which the combination will increase the amount of local news in the market; whether each media outlet in the combination will exercise independent news judgement; the level of concentration in the DMA [Designated Market Area]; the financial condition of the newspaper or TV station, and whether the new owner plans to invest in newsroom operation if either outlet is in financial distress (FCC, 2008, June 24, italics added).
2. *Mike Duffy* soon went off the air when the show's host and namesake was given a Senate appointment by Prime Minister Stephen Harper. The program was renamed *Power Play*. In June 2009, Don Newman retired and his show was renamed *Power and Politics*. Initially both programs maintained similar formats—interviewing journalists in panel segments.
3. In 2008, the CTRC levelled the corporate playing field by releasing Quebecor from its earlier commitment to maintain separate newsrooms (CRTC,

2008–5). There could have been conditions applied to the licence renewals of Canwest and CTV. Some have speculated that the smaller and more concentrated market in Quebec, as well as heightened sensitivity to the potential impact of cross-ownership, also played a role in differing requirements.

4. In the event of multiple newspaper stories, the "most similar" one was selected for the comparison. For the English-language study, the researchers used transcripts of TV news programs that were available either directly through ProQuest or through subscription from the Virtual News Library. However, the taped stories were kept for additional investigation and qualitative analysis. The French-language study developed a multimedia online coding system, using an automatic digital recording device, then integrating video files and text of print articles into FileMaker Pro to facilitate comparison.

5. The technique of *paired comparison* appears to have been first used by Everett Rogers in his seminal study of diffusion of information (1962). For other studies using the method, see Albers-Miller, 1966; Sutcliffe et al., 2009.

3 Content-Sharing in National Media

1. In the French-language sample, coders found some shared content in the form of opinion polls published in both Quebecor media, as well as occasional use of video images in the newspaper.

2. Canwest served its one-year notice in June 2006 that it would leave CP in order to focus on its in-house Canwest News Service (Trichur, 2006). At the time, *Edmonton Journal* Editor-in-Chief Allan Mayer noted that Canwest had already reduced the number of photos and stories taken from the wire service. He argued, "[t]his move could ultimately allow us to provide readers with enhanced coverage from different news sources" (*Edmonton Journal*, 2006, June 29). In our sample of paired comparisons, we found only one *National Post* story that came from the CP wire, despite the fact that the relationship did not terminate until June 2007, midway through our study.

   Of course, Canwest no longer survives as a "converged company." However, Quebecor served notice to CP in the summer of 2009 that it would leave the news cooperative in a year's time. In our view, the "corporate news service model" will be used by Quebecor to promote content-sharing among all media platforms owned by the company. How much TV-newspaper sharing will result is open to debate (see chapters 5 and 6, this volume).

3. While the original similarity measures were ordinal level measures and hence were appropriately analyzed using cross-tabulations (and related statistics), the similarity index or average similarity score could be conceived of as interval level. Since interval data often produce more informative results, we re-analyzed the summary similarity index in its interval form (without recoding to appropriate constituent scales), using a t-test (with the test and control groups as the independent variables). The results confirm the cross-tabulation analysis (data not shown). We also performed a parallel analysis of variance for the index variables in chapter 4, with the three groups (Edmonton TV and newspaper, Canwest national TV and newspaper and CBC-TV, and Halifax/Winnipeg newspaper control groups) as the independent variables. Again, the results confirmed the tabular analysis.
4. In attempting to assess the general applicability of these findings, we must first acknowledge that content-sharing might well have been more likely to occur in the context of election coverage. We had indeed made plans to add two weeks of election coverage to our sample if a federal election had been called in 2007. In spite of intense speculation, a federal election did not take place until the fall of 2008, well beyond the time during which we were collecting data. Thus, the possibility remains that for selected events such as elections, the barriers to content-sharing for multitasking journalists may be less robust, and consequently more shared content would appear.

4 Content-Sharing in English-Language Local Market Media

1. Canwest's withdrawal from Canadian Press did not take place until July 2007.

5 Media Executives Assess the Impact of Convergence and New Media

1. For many of our respondents who worked in media in various capacities, ownership was a sensitive issue and we assured them confidentiality. Because the pool of respondents was small, especially when divided by language, in order to guarantee confidentiality, we decided not to reveal the names and organizations of any of those we interviewed.

    At the beginning of our interview with Lise Lareau, president of the Canadian Media Guild (see chapter 6, this volume), she observed that Canadian media were in a "period of non-self-examination" with respect to journalistic practice. "People are not asking, 'What are we doing wrong?'" (interview, 2009, Sept. 3). An ongoing survey of Canadian daily newspaper editors on reporting of international news appears to confirm this view: in the first survey conducted in 1988, over 50 per cent of editors responded; this percentage declined in each of the three surveys that followed, bottoming out at just over 15 per cent in 2006 (Sutcliffe et al., 2009).

2. There is, of course, a history behind the Canwest News Service—namely the Southam News Service that existed in the days prior to Conrad Black's purchase of the Southam chain of newspapers. Postmedia Network Canada Corp., the successor company to Canwest in the newspaper business, appears to have continued with the corporate news service model, renaming it the "Postmedia News Service."

3. Quebecor has also attempted to consolidate its resources at the Quebec National Assembly under the umbrella of its corporate news service, QMI. As of this writing (fall 2010), Sun Media had been unsuccessful in challenging QNA President Yvon Vallières's decision to withhold accreditation from two journalists from the *Journal de Québec*. Granting this accreditation, according to the association of journalists in the parliamentary press gallery, would have violated the principle of neutrality regarding labour disputes. The Quebec Superior Court ruled in favour of the QNA president, asserting that it was "not up to judges to determine how this parliamentary privilege is practiced" (*Montreal Gazette*, 2010, Sept. 22).

4. Both newspaper and TV properties of Quebecor did in fact leave CP in the summer of 2010.

5. In Canada, conventional television broadcasters air content and it is picked up free of charge by consumers who can get the signal by means of a conventional antenna. Cable companies also pick up the signal free of charge and retransmit to their customers for a fee. The "fee for carriage" debate centres on whether cable companies should pay the conventional broadcasters for use of their signals. In that cable companies are financially successful while conventional broadcasters are under stress, the latter, including the CBC, asked the CRTC for a change in the rules. In a March 2010 decision, the CRTC allowed private broadcasters (but not the CBC/SRC) to negotiate signal fees with cable companies, but declined to impose regulations, leaving things in the hands of the markets and the courts (see Vieira and Sturgeon, 2010, Mar. 23).

6 Stakeholders Assess the State of Canadian Media

1. Debt appears to have been the major source of Canwest's problems as well.
2. In 2009, The Canadian Press, a non-profit co-op, "began looking for investors to take an ownership stake in what would become a for-profit business....to temporarily relieve its financial burdens,...CP obtained federal approval to delay payments to make up a $35-million deficit in its pension plans, from 2009 until 2011" (Krashinsky, 2010, Apr. 28). In early July 2010, it was reported that a deal had been struck that would see CP privatized under the ownership of "its three largest members"—CTVglobemedia, Torstar and Gesca (Krashinsky, 2010, July 4).
3. Recent collective agreements at *La Presse* and Radio-Canada affirm the reality of multitasking, with the incorporation of web practices. Journalists will no longer work exclusively on the print edition of the newspaper or conventional broadcasting media but will also produce online content in audio, video and textual form. Additional compensation will be offered in some cases.
4. In the course of our interview with Lareau, she shared with us a *Toronto Sun Family: 1971–2009* blog entry. An internal memo suggested that Quebecor was already cutting its ties with CP: "It has become increasingly evident that our relationship with Canadian Press is rapidly deteriorating, it's therefore imperative that we eliminate CP completely from our editorial line-ups." The blogger responded: "Pardon us if we sound like a broken record, but we doubt QMI will ever fill the CP void with Sun Media newsrooms operating as they are with minimal employees and on shoestring budgets." An anonymous commenter added, "So basically if Sun Media didn't cover it, it didn't happen I guess is what they're saying. We'll just write a column about it a day or two later" (as quoted in *Toronto Sun Family*, 2009, Aug. 21). A Quebec newspaper executive indicated as well that for Sun Media, the "convergence logic was in full force" (interview, 2009, June 17, translated by Colette Brin). A possible wild card in the trend toward corporate news services is, of course, the ownership connection between CTVglobemedia and Thomson-owned Reuters news service. In our interviews, we were unable to unearth any information that would suggest that this connection would likely be exploited.

7 Old Media, New Media, Any Media?

1. In attempting to assess the general applicability of these findings, we must first acknowledge that content-sharing might well have been more likely to occur in the context of election campaign coverage. As previously mentioned, we had indeed made plans to add two weeks of election coverage to our sample if a federal election had been called in 2007.

    We reiterate our major finding that as of 2007, content-sharing among television and newspaper properties of major Canadian media corporations was certainly not an established practice and, as a senior television news editor told us in an e-mail, these "findings are as we might have expected" (e-mail correspondence, 2009, Sept. 15). A Quebec newspaper executive likewise agreed that our results reflected accurately the situation with respect to content-sharing in 2007. He also indicated that had the study been done in 2009, there would have been similar findings, but that by 2011, there would perhaps be significantly more content-sharing: his view was that "change is coming, but not yet" (interview, 2009, June 17, translated by Colette Brin).

2. Some work in this area has already begun. In a related study, Miljan (2008) examined the *Toronto Star*'s 2008 federal election coverage. She compared the paper's online edition with its daily print edition to determine, in part, what effect if any the most recent *Toronto Star* collective agreement had on journalistic practice. In that the new contract changed the definition of *journalist* to "anyone who generates content," there was a concern that the *Star*'s reporters would become two-way or even three-way reporters. However, contrary to expectations, the study showed that conventional journalistic roles remained quite stable despite the change in contract language. Miljan's conclusion was that the old rules regarding what it means to be a journalist overrode the new expectations contained in the contract and that the entrenched routines and norms that differentiated writers from photographers continued to hold. Journalists reported that they could not shoot video or take pictures that they considered of high enough quality to be put on websites or appear in the print edition of the paper. Instead they continued to focus on their main goal, which was to get the story out. Our assessment is that there will be a change in newsroom routines, but that these will occur gradually as new multiplatform-trained reporters come on stream.

3. At a presentation of our findings to the 2010 Canadian Communication Association Meeting in Montreal, a seasoned newspaper journalist turned academic summed up his feelings after having experimented with the broadcast format: "There's a reason why some of us are in print."

4. There are two major problems in dealing with news that is not covered. The first involves identifying what actually is newsworthy and not covered by mainstream news organizations, and the second is that what is missing may not necessarily be a result of an ownership conspiracy but rather a product of a conventional news selection (see NewsWatch Canada, 2010; Herman and Chomsky, 1988).
5. As of early October 2009, CBC took the position that, along with Canwest Global and CTVglobemedia, it too should be paid a "fee for carriage" by cable companies retransmitting its programming (see "ON AIR: Cable's Dirty Little Secret," 2009, Oct. 6). The CRTC in its 2010 ruling did not agree.

   Also of interest in terms of content-sharing, in October 2009 the CBC and Canwest's flagship newspaper the *National Post* announced a content-sharing agreement wherein the CBC "will run daily financial stories and podcasts from the *Post*. The *Post*, in turn, will run daily CBC sports stories on its website and occasionally in the newspaper's print edition" (Reuters, 2009, Oct. 2: B4). Of course, Canwest, which at the time of the agreement was still the owner of the *National Post*, also owned a television network and a website that competed directly with the CBC.

Postscript

1. It should be noted that Quebecor already operates an all-news channel in French, Le Canal Nouvelles (LCN).

References

Akin, David. (2009, Apr. 25). "Most newspapers still profitable but business evolving." *The Windsor Star*, A1.

———. (2009, Apr. 27). "Advertisers still bullish on print." *The Windsor Star*, C8.

———. (2009, Apr. 28). "Canada's newspapers hold their own." *The Windsor Star*, C7.

Albers-Miller, Nancy. (1996). "Designing Cross-cultural Advertising Research: A Closer Look at Paired Comparisons." *International Marketing Review* 13 (5): 59–75.

Anderson, Benedict. (1991). *Imagined Communities: Reflections on the Origin and Spread of Nationalism*. Rev. ed. London and New York: Verso.

Arab, Paula. (2001, July 2). "CRTC ruling to set path of convergence." *Toronto Star*. Retrieved July 15, 2010, from http://www.friends.ca/news-item/3981.

Asper, Leonard. (2001). "Observations on the Media, Canada and Winnipeg." *Canadian Speeches* 14 (6): 54. Retrieved Feb. 14, 2008, from CBCA Reference database. (Document ID: 374783161).

Austen, Ian. (2010, Jan. 10). "CanWest newspaper unit files for bankruptcy." *The New York Times*. Retrieved Feb. 16, 2010, from http://www.nytimes.com/2010/01/09/business/media/09paper.html.

Avilés, José, and Miguel Carvajal. (2008). "Integrated and Cross-media Newsroom Convergence: Two Models of Multimedia News Production: The Cases of Novotécnica and La Verdad Multimedia in Spain." *Convergence* 14 (2): 221–239.

Avilés, José, Klaus Meier, Andy Kaltenbrunner, Miguel Carvajal, and Daniela Kraus. (2009). "Newsroom Integration in Austria, Spain and Germany: Models of Media Convergence." *Journalism Practice* 3 (3): 285–303.

Bagdikian, Ben. (2004). *The New Media Monopoly*. Boston: Beacon Press.

Baker, Edwin. (2007). *Media Concentration and Democracy: Why Ownership Matters*. Cambridge: Cambridge University Press.

Balingall, Robert. (2006). "Black Consciousness and the Canadian Media's Portrayal of the Third World." *Undercurrent* 3 (2): 52–59.

Bass, Alan. (2009, Aug. 26). E-mail correspondence.

BCE. (2006, Dec. 14). "Bell Globemedia changes name to CTVglobemedia effective January 1, 2007." Retrieved July 4, 2008, from http://www.bce.ca/en/news/releases/bg/2006/12/14/74071.html.

Benedetti, Paul, Tim Currie, and Kim Kierans. (2010). *The New Journalist: Roles, Skills, and Critical Thinking*. Toronto: Edmond Montgomery.

Bernier, Marc-François. (2008). *Journalistes au pays de la convergence: Sérénité, malaise et détresse dans la profession*. Québec: Presses de l'Université Laval.

Bousquet, Richard. (2002). "La convergence et le déficit démocratique." 2001 Bogues. Globalisme et pluralisme. Conference proceedings. Retrieved Feb. 12, 2010, from www.er.uquam.ca/noble/gricis/actes/bogues/Bousquet.pdf.

Brent, Paul. (2005, Jan. 26). "Newspapers here to stay, panel says." *Financial Post*, FP6.

Bruser, David. (2005, Dec. 3). "Media map rewritten as Torstar buys into rival." *Saturday Star*, A1.

Business Week. (2004, July 12). "The Dangers of Media Mergers." Editorial. Retrieved July 15, 2010, from http://www.businessweek.com/print/magazine.content/04_28/b3891166_mz029.htm.

Butterworth, Trevor (2010, Mar. 31). "The Future of Journalism." *Forbes*. Retrieved May 5, 2010, from http://www.forbes.com/2010/03/30/journalism-media-digital-internet-opinions-columnists-trevor-butterworth.html.

Cameron, Daphné. (2011, Apr. 4). "Pas de bousculade pour revenir au Journal de Montréal." Retrieved Apr. 12, 2011, from http://lapresseaffaires.cyberpresse.ca/economie/medias-et-telecoms/201104/04/01-4386232-pas-de-bousculade-pour-revenir-au-journal-de-montreal.php.

Canada. (1965). *Report of the Committee on Broadcasting*. Ottawa: Queen's Printer.

———. (1970). *Report of the Special Senate Committee on Mass Media. Vol. 1, The Uncertain Mirror*. Ottawa: Information Canada.

———. (1978). *Report of the Royal Commission on Corporate Concentration*. Ottawa: Supply and Services.

———. (1981). Royal Commission on Newspapers. *Report of the Royal Commission on Newspapers*. Ottawa: Supply and Services.

———. (1986). *Report of the Task Force on Broadcast Policy*. Ottawa: Supply and Services.

———. (2004). Senate, Standing Committee on Transport and Communications. *Interim Report on the Canadian News Media*. Retrieved July 15, 2010, from http://www.parl.gc.ca/37/3/parlbus.commbus/senate/com-e/tran-e/rep04apr04-e.htm.

———. (2006). Senate, Standing Committee on Transport and Communications. *Final Report on the Canadian News Media*. Retrieved July 15, 2010, from http://www.parl.gc.ca/39/1/parlbus/commbus/senate/com-e/tran-e/rep-e/repfinjun06 vol1-e.htm.

Canadian Internet Project (CIP-RIC). (2008, Sept. 24). "Canadian Internet Project launches report from second phase of study on Canadian Internet habits." Retrieved July 15, 2010, from http://www.newswire.ca/en/story/255593/canadian-internet-project-launches-report-from-second-phase-of-study-on-canadian-internet-habits.

Canadian Media Research Consortium. (2004). "Report Card on Canadian News Media." Retrieved July 15, 2010, from http://www.cmrcccrm.ca/english/reportcard2004/01html.

Canadian Press (CP). (2009, Mar. 2). "CTV Fears for A Channel Survival." *CARDonline*. Retrieved Sept. 22, 2009, from http://www.marketingmag.ca.english/news/media/article.jsp?content=20090227_174817_4732.

"CanWest eyes withdrawal from Canadian Press in favour of developing internal news coverage." (2006, June 29). *Edmonton Journal* [Final Edition]. Retrieved Feb. 26, 2008, from http://www.proquest.com.ezproxy.uwindsor.ca/.

Carlin, Vince. (2003). "No Clear Channel: The Rise and Possible Fall of Media Convergence." In D. Taras, F. Pannekoek, and M. Bakardjieva (eds.). *How Canadians Communicate*. Calgary, AB: University of Calgary Press, 51–69.

CBC. (2001, Aug. 2). "Conditions attached to new CTV, Global licences." Retrieved July 15, 2010, from http://cbc.ca/canada/story/2001/08/02/crtc010802.html.

———. (2007). *CBC Annual Report 2006–07*. Ottawa: Corporate Communications.

Centre d'études sur les médias. (n.d.). "Aperçu des règles des débats relatifs a la concentration des médias." Retrieved July 15, 2010, from http://www.cem.ulaval.ca/concentration_medias/.

———. (2010). "Comment les Québécois s'informent-ils?" Centre d'études sur les médias.

Chase, Steven. (2010, June 11). "'Fox News North' sets bait for reporters." *The Globe and Mail*, A7.

Chomsky, Daniel. (2006). "'An Interested Reader': Measuring Ownership Control at the New York Times." *Critical Studies in Media Communication* 23 (1): 1–18.

Clarke, Debra. (2005). "Audience Experiences of Convergence." In David Skinner, James Compton, and Michael Gasher (eds.). *Converging Media, Diverging Politics: A political Economy of news media in the United States and Canada*. Toronto: Rowman & Littlefield, 165–186.

Clement, Wallace. (1975). *The Canadian Corporate Elite: An Analysis of Economic Power*. Toronto: McClelland & Stewart.

Cohen, Bernard. (1963). *The Press and Foreign Policy*. Princeton, NJ: Princeton University Press.

Collard, Nathalie. (2010, May 21). "Les journalistes de la première chaîne craignent de perdre leur identité." *La Presse*. Retrieved from http://www.cyberpresse.ca/arts/medias/201005/21/01-4282622-les-journalistes-de-la-premiere-chaine-craignent-de-perdre-leur-identite.php.

Commission on Freedom of the Press. (1947). *A Free and Responsible Press. A General Report on Mass Communication: Newspapers, Radio, Motion Picture, Magazines and Books*. Chicago: University of Chicago Press.

Compaine, Benjamin, and Douglas Gomery. (2000). *Who Owns the Media? Competition and Concentration in the Mass Media Industry*. 3rd ed. Mahwah, NJ: Lawrence Erlbaum Associates.

CRTC. (2008-02-11). "Canwest Corporate structure," #14 Ownership Broadcasting, CRTC.

———. (2008-4). "Broadcasting Public Notice CRTC 2008-4: Diversity of Voices." Canadian Radio-television and Telecommunications Commission, 15 January. Retrieved July 15, 2010, from http://www.crtc.gc.ca/archive/eng/archive/2008/pb2008-4.htm.

———. (2008-5). "Broadcasting Public Notice CRTC 2008-5: Journalistic Independence Code. Canadian Radio-television and Telecommunications Commission, 15 January. Retrieved July 15, 2010, from http://www.crtc.gc.ca/archive/eng/archive/2008/pb2008-5.htm.

Dacruz, Michelle. (2004, Mar. 25). "CanWest reaffirms convergence plan." *Financial Post*, FP7.

Dahl, Robert. (1989). *Democracy and Its Critics*. New Haven, CT: Yale University Press.

Dailey, Larry, Lori Demo, and Mary Spillman. (2005a). "The Convergence Continuum: A Model for Studying Collaboration Between Media Newsrooms." *Atlantic Journal of Communication* 13 (3): 150–168.

———. (2005b). "Most TV/Newspapers Partners at Cross Promotion Stage." *Newspaper Research Journal* 26 (4): 36–49.

Desplanques, Anne Caroline. (2011, Apr. 5). "Péladeau sur le JdeM: le syndicat n'a pas compris l'évolution du marché." *ProjetJ.ca*. Retrieved Apr. 12, 2011, from http://projetj.ca/article/peladeau-sur-le-jdem-le-syndicat-na-pas-compris-levolution-du-marche.

Deutsch, Karl. (1954). *Political Community at the International Level: Problems of Definition and Measurement*. Garden City, NY: Doubleday.

Dixon, Guy. (2008, Feb. 21). "New duties for CBC-TV and Radio bosses." *The Globe and Mail*, R3.

Dixon, Guy, and James Bradshaw. (2009, Oct. 31). "Mother Corp. gussies up her all-news baby." *The Globe and Mail*, R7.

Duhe, Sonya Forte, with Melissa Mortimer and Sand San Chow. (2004). "Convergence in North American TV Newsrooms: A Nationwide Look." *Convergence* 10 (2): 81–104.

Durocher, Sophie. (2010, May 5). "Ici Radio-Gesca." *24 heures*. Retrieved Nov. 13, 2010, from http://fr.canoe.ca/cgi-bin/imprimer.cgi?id=660856.

Edge, Marc. (2005). "Convergence and the 'Black News Hole': Canadian Newspaper Coverage of the 2003 Lincoln Report." Paper presented at the annual meeting of the Canadian Communication Association, London, Ontario.

———. (2007). *Asper Nation: Canada's Most Dangerous Media Company*. Vancouver: New Star Books.

Edmonton Journal [Final Edition]. (2006, June 29). "Canwest eyes withdrawal from Canadian Press in favour of developing internal news coverage." Retrieved June 29, 2008, from http://www.proquest.com.ezproxy.uwindsor.ca/.

Entman, Robert. (1993) "Framing: Towards a Clarification of a Fractured Paradigm." *Journal of Communication* 43: 51–58.

———. (2004) *Projections of Power: Framing News, Public Opinion, and U.S. Foreign Policy*. Chicago: University of Chicago Press.

FCC (Federal Communications Commission). (2008, June 24). "FCC's Review of the Broadcast Ownership Rules." Retrieved July 15, 2010, from http://www.fcc.gov/cbg/consumerfacts/reviewrules.html.

Field, Terry. (2009, Aug. 25)."Rupert Murdoch: news savior." *Winnipeg Free Press*, A10.

Filak, Vincent. (2004) "Cultural Convergence: Intergroup Bias Among Journalists and its Impact on Convergence." *Atlantic Journal of Communication* 12 (4): 216–232.

Financial Post. (2009, Sept. 5). "Canwest Sells Victoria TV station." *Financial Post*. Retrieved Sept. 20, 2009, from http://www.straight.com/article-254996/canwest-sells-chektv-employees-and-victoria-investors.

Flavelle, Dana, and John Spears. (2010, Feb. 12). "Shaw buys control of Canwest Global." Retrieved July 15, 2010, from http://www.thestar.com/business.article/764426—shaw-buys-control-of-canwest global.

Fleras, Angie. (2001). "Couched in Compromise: Media-Minority Relations in a Multicultural Society." In C. McKie and B. Singer (eds.). *Communication in Canadian Society*. 5th ed. Toronto: Thompson Educational Publishing, 308–322.

Fletcher, Frederick J. (1981). *The Newspaper and Public Affairs: Vol. 7. Research Studies on the Newspaper Industry*. Ottawa: Supply and Services.

Gans, Herbert (2010). "News & the News Media in the Digital Age: Implications for Democracy." *Daedalus* 139 (2): 8–17.

George, Eric. (2007). "Problématiser les liens entre la concentration des industries de la communication et le pluralisme de l'information." In Philippe Bouquillion and Yolande Combes (eds.). *Les industries de la culture et de la communication en mutation*. Paris: L'Harmattan, 33–44.

Gestin, Philippe, Christopher Gimbert, Florence Le Cam, Magali Rodhomme-Allègre, Yvon Rochard, Hélène Romeyer, and Denis Ruellan. (2009). "La production multisupports dans des groupes médiatiques français: premières remarques." *Les Cahiers du journalisme* 20: 84–95.

Ghanem, Salma. (1997). "Filing in the Tapestry: The Second Level of Agenda Setting." In M. McCombs, D. Shaw, and D. Weaver (eds.). *Communication and Democracy: Exploring the Intellectual Frontiers in Agenda-Setting Theory*. Mahwah, NJ: Lawrence Erlbaum Associates, 3–14.

Gingras, Anne-Marie. (2006). *Médias et démocratie*. 2nd ed. Québec: Presses de l'Université du Québec.

Goldstein, Kenneth. (2002). *Fragmentation, Consolidation and the Canadian Consumer*. Winnipeg, MB: Communications Management Inc.

———. (2004). "From Assumptions of Scarcity to the Facts of Fragmentation: The Impact on Public Policies and Private Business Models for the Media." Paper presented at the conference, "How Canadians Communicate," University of Calgary.

———. (2009). "Remarks" presented to the "Ink and Beyond" Conference, Canadian Newspaper Association, Montreal. Winnipeg, MB: Communications Management Inc.

———. (2009, Aug. 25). Interview.

Gordon, Rich. (2003). "The Meanings and Implications of Convergence." In K. Kawamoto (ed.). *Digital Journalism: Emerging Media and the Changing Horizons of Journalism*. Latham, MD: Rowman and Littlefield, 57–74.

Gormley, William. (1976). *The Effects of Newspaper-Television Cross-Ownership on News Hegemony*. Chapel Hill, NC: Institute for Research in Social Science, University of North Carolina.

Hackett, Robert, and Yeuzhi Zhao. (1998). *Sustaining Democracy? Journalism and the Politics of Objectivity*. Toronto: Garamond Press.

Herman, Edward, and Noam Chomsky. (1988). *Manufacturing Consent: The Political Economy of the Mass Media*. New York: Pantheon Books.

Holsti, Ole R. (1969). *Content Analysis for the Social Sciences and Humanities*. Reading, MA: Addison-Wesley.

Horwitz, Robert. (2005). "On Media Concentration and the Diversity Question." *The Information Society* 21 (3): 181–204.

Huang, Edgar, Lisa Rademakers, Moshood Fayemiwo, and Lillian Dunlap. (2004). "Converged Journalism and Quality: A Case Study of The Tampa Tribune News Stories." *Convergence: The International Journal of Research into New Media Technologies* 10 (4): 73–91.

Interview. (2009, May 29). Canadian politician.

———. (2009, June 16). Quebec newspaper journalist. Translated by Colette Brin.

———. (2009, June 17). Quebec newspaper executive. Translated by Colette Brin.

———. (2009a, June 18). Quebec television executive. Translated by Colette Brin.

———. (2009b, June 18). Canadian government policy analysts (joint interview).

———. (2009, June 22). Quebec journalist. Translated by Colette Brin.

———. (2009, Aug. 24). Canadian daily newspaper editor.

———. (2009, Aug. 26). Canadian daily newspaper editor.

———. (2009, Aug. 27). Canadian television executive.

———. (2009, Sept. 1). Canadian daily newspaper publisher.

———. (2009, Sept. 16). Former Canadian journalist.

———. (2009, Sept. 22). Senior Canadian media executive.

———. (2009, Sept. 24). Quebec media regulators (joint interview). Translated by Colette Brin.

———. (2009, Oct. 1). Quebec media regulator. Translated by Colette Brin.

———. (2010, Jan. 27). Quebec newspaper journalist. Translated by Colette Brin.

———. (2010, Feb. 15). Quebec media executive. Translated by Colette Brin.

Iyengar, Shanto. (1991). *Is Anyone Responsible?: How Television Frames Political Issues*. Chicago: University of Chicago Press.

Jackson, Joseph (1999, Dec. 17). *Newspaper Ownership in Canada: An Overview of the Davey Committee and Kent Commission Studies*. Government of Canada. Retrieved July 15, 2010, from http://dsp-psd.pwgsc.ca/Collection-R/LoP/BdB/prb9935-e.htm.

Jedwab, Jack. (2003, Feb. 10). "Canadian Media: Trust, Bias and Control." Poll conducted by Environics Research for the conference, "Who Controls Canada's Media?" McGill University.

Jodoin, Simon. (2010, May 11). "Sophie Durocher, La Presse et Radio-Canada: les malheurs de Sophie." *BangBang*. Retrieved Nov. 13, 2010, from http://bangbangblog.com/sophie-durocher-la-presse-et-radio-canada-les-malheurs-de-sophie/.

Kalb, Marvin, and Amy Sullivan. (2000). "Editorial: Media Mergers: 'Bigger Is Better' Isn't Necessarily Better." *The Harvard International Journal of Press/Politics* 5 (2): 1–5.

Ketterer, Stan, Tom Wier, Steven Smethers, and James Back. (2004). "Case Study Shows Limited Benefits of Convergence." *Newspaper Research Journal* 25 (3): 52–65.

Khan, Saleem. (2002, Apr. 26). "'Unapologetically Pro-Israel' Canwest Imposes National Editorials on Local Papers." *The Washington Report on Middle East Affairs*.

Kimber, Stephen. (2008, Feb. 24). "The Halifax Daily News: 1974–2008." Center for Journalism Ethics, School of Journalism and Mass Communication, University of Wisconsin-Madison. Retrieved July 15, 2010, from http://www.journalismethics.ca/feature_articles/halifax_daily_news.html.

Knox, Paul. (2008). "Not in the Newsroom...: Free Expression and Media Concentration in Canada: The Case of Canwest Global." *The Round Table: The Commonwealth Journal of International Affairs* 91 (320): 503–520.

Kosicki, Gerald. (1993). "Problems and Opportunities in Agenda Setting Research." *Journal of Communication* 43 (2): 100–127.

Kraepling, Camile, and Anna Criado. (2006). "Survey Shows TV/Newspapers Maintaining Partnerships." *Newspaper Research Journal* 27 (4): 52–65.

Krashinsky, Susan. (2009, Oct. 3). "Lights dim for last time at small Manitoba station." *The Globe and Mail*, B5.

———. (2010, Apr. 28). "CP, media firms push on with restructuring efforts." *The Globe and Mail*, B9.

———. (2010, July 4). "Tentative deal set to transform Canadian Press news service." *The Globe and Mail*. Retrieved July 7, 2010, from http://www.theglobeandmail.com/report-on-business/media-companies-strike-deal-for-canadian-press/article1627908/.

———. (2010, Sept. 11). "The CTV deal: Torstar's exit 'a great opportunity.'" *The Globe and Mail*, B8.

———. (2010, Oct. 5). "Sun TV gears down licence application." *The Globe and Mail*. Retrieved Nov. 13, 2010, from http://www.theglobeandmail.com/globe-investor/sun-tv-gears-down-licence-application/article1743859.

Krashinsky, Susan, and Grant Robertson. (2010, May 4). "Shaw shakes up TV sector with CanWest deal." *The Globe and Mail*, B1.

Lareau, Lise. (2009, Sept. 3). Interview.

Lavoie, Marie-Hélène. (2004). "Media Cross-Ownership in Canada." *Media Studies*. Canadian Heritage. Retrieved Mar. 12, 2005, from http://pch.gc.ca/progs/ac-caprogs/esm-ms/crois6_e.cfm.

Lawson-Borders, Grace. (2006). *Media Organizations and Convergence: Case Studies of Media Convergence Pioneers*. Mahwah, NJ: Lawrence Erlbaum Associates.

Lemay, Marie-France-Lou. (2008, May 9). "Entente décriée et contestée à Radio-Canada." *Journal de Montréal*. Retrieved Feb. 12, 2010, from http://fr.canoe.ca/divertissement/tele-medias/nouvelles/2008/05/09/5517196-jdm.html.

Locke, John. (1965). *Two Treatises of Government*. New York: New American Library.

Lowrey, Wilson. (2006). "Cognitive Shortcuts, the Constraints of Commitment, and Managers' Attitudes About Newspaper-TV Partnerships." *Journal of Media Economics* 19 (4): 241–258.

Lowry, Tom, Ronald Grover, Catherine Yang, Steve Rosenbush, and Peter Burrows. (2004, Feb. 23). "Mega Media Mergers: How Dangerous?" *Business Week*. Retrieved July 15, 2010, from http://www.businessweek.com/print.magazine/content/04_08/b3871001_mz001.htm.

Luft, Oliver. (2008, June 27). "Growth of news sites harming investment in news gathering, says Lords report." *Online Journalism News*. Retrieved July 15, 2010, from http://www.journalism.co.uk/2/articles/531831.php.

Luzadder, Dan. (2003). "Canadian Media Deregulation Provides Insight into FCC Proposal." AUSC *Annenberg Online Journalism Review* 06–10. Retrieved July 15, 2010, from http://www.ojr.org/ojr/law/1054219939.php.

Marlow, Ian. (2010, June 9). "On foreign ownership rules and the competition." *The Globe and Mail*, B5.

———. (2010, Sept. 10). "Vidéotron's wireless launch being built on content." *The Globe and Mail*. Retrieved Nov. 13, 2010, from http://www.theglobeandmail.com/globe-investor/videotrons-wireless-launch-being-built-on-content/article1701104.

———. (2010, Sept. 11). "BELL'S BIG BET: The $1.3-billion return of convergence." *The Globe and Mail*, B1.

Marotte, Bertrand. (2009, Sept. 4). "La Presse demands concessions from staff." *The Globe and Mail*, B3.

Martin, Lawrence. (2010, Aug. 19). "Is Stephen Harper set to move against the CRTC?" *The Globe and Mail*, A15.

Martini, Megan. (2010, July 6). "Quebecor's press council withdrawal affects credibility." *The Gazette*. Retrieved July 15, 2010, from http://www.montrealgazette.com/news/Quebecor+press+council+withdrawal+affects+credibility/3242906/story.htm.

McChesney, Robert. (2000). *Rich Media, Poor Democracy: Communication Politics in Dubious Times*. New York: The New Press.

McCombs, Maxwell. (2005). "A Look at Agenda-Setting: Past, Present and Future." *Journalism Studies* 6: 543–557.

McCombs, Maxwell, and Amy Reynolds. (2002). "News Influence on Our Pictures of the World." In J. Bryant and D. Zilman (eds.). *Media Effects: Advances in Theory and Research*. 2nd ed. Mahwah, NJ: Lawrence Erlbaum Associates, 1–18.

McCombs, Maxwell, and Donald Shaw. (1993). "The Evolution of Agenda-Setting Research: Twenty-Five Years in the Marketplace of Ideas." *Journal of Communication* 43: 58–67.

McQuail, Denis. (1992). *Media Performance: Mass Communication and the Public Interest*. Beverly Hills, CA: Sage.

Merrill, John. (1974). *The Imperative of Freedom: A Philosophy of Journalistic Autonomy*. New York: Hastings House.

———. (2009, June 23). E-mail correspondence.

Meyer, Philip. (2009). *The Vanishing Newspaper: Saving Journalism in the Information Age*. 2nd ed. Columbia: University of Missouri Press.

Miliband, Ralph. (1969). *The State in Capitalist Society*. London: Weidenfeld and Nicolson.

Miljan, Lydia. (2008). "Convergence Journalism: A Threat to Print Journalism?" Paper presented at the Centre for International Media Analysis, Research and Consultancy Conference, Lutton, England.

Mill, John Stuart. (1955). *On Liberty*. Chicago: Henry Regnery.

Miller, John. (1998). *Yesterday's News: Why Canada's Newspapers Are Failing Us*. Halifax, NS: Fernwood Press.

Millette, Lise. (2010, Oct.). "QMI: Dans l'antre de la bête." *Trente*, 29–32.

Mills, Russell. (2003, Feb. 13–15). "To What Extent Can or Should Media Owners Intervene in Content?" Paper presented at the conference, "Who Controls Canada's Media?" McGill University.

Milton, John. (1971). *Areopagitica*. New York: AMS Press.

Mongeau, Natacha, and Fernand Amesse. (2001). "La propriété croisée entre types de médias: contexte industriel, stratégie d'entreprise et diversité de l'information." In *La propriété croisée des médias au Canada*. Rapport présenté par le Centre d'études sur les médias au CRTC et au ministère du Patrimoine canadien, 18–21. Available in English translation; retrieved July 15, 2010, from http://www.cem.ulaval.ca/TDM_concCROISE.html.

Montreal Gazette. (2010, Sept. 22). "Judge upholds press gallery accreditation veto." *Montreal Gazette*. Retrieved Nov. 13, 2010, from http://www.montrealgazette.com/news/Judge+upholds+press+gallery+accreditation+veto/3562473/story.html.

Moore, Aaron. (2002). "Ownership: A Chill in Canada." *Columbia Journalism Review* 40 (6): 1–11.

msnbc. (2009, Dec. 3). "GE reaches deal with Comcast for NBC." Retrieved July 15, 2010, from http://www.msn.com/id/34247302/.

Murray, Simone. (2003). "Media Convergence's Third Wave: Content Streaming." *Convergence: The International Journal of Research into New Media Technologies* 9 (1): 8–18.

Nesbitt-Larking, Paul. (2001). *Politics, Society and the Media: Canadian Perspectives*. Peterborough, ON: Broadview Press.

NewsWatch Canada. Retrieved Nov. 15, 2010, from http://sfu.ca/cmns/research/newswatch/intro.html.

Olive, David. (2007, May 5). "Thomson bid sure to face obstacles: financial data juggernaut." Retrieved July 15, 2010, from http://www.thestar.com/Business/article/210704.

"ON AIR: Cable's Dirty Little Secret." (2009, Oct. 6). (Advertisement). *The Globe and Mail*, Section A.

Page, Benjamin I. (1996). *Who Deliberates?: Mass Media in Modern Democracy*. Chicago: University of Chicago Press.

Peers, Frank. (1969). *The Politics of Canadian Broadcasting, 1920–1951*. Toronto: University of Toronto Press.

Picard, Robert. (1985). *The Press and the Decline of Democracy: The Democratic Socialist Response in Public Policy*. Westport, CT: Greenwood Press.

Picard, Robert, James Winter, Maxwell McCombs, and Stephen Lacy. (1988). *Press Concentration and Monopoly: New Perspectives on Newspaper Ownership and Operation*. Norwood, NJ: Ablex Publishing Corporation.

Pitts, Gordon. (2002). *Kings of Convergence: The Fight for Control of Canada's Media*. Toronto: Doubleday.

———. (2005, Dec. 3). "The new landscape: more deals in the works." *The Globe and Mail*, B5.

———. (2009, Oct. 7). "Izzy's vision, Leonard's woes." *The Globe and Mail*, B1.

———. (2010, Sept. 11). "Sale of CTV a redemption for vision of convergence." *The Globe and Mail*, B4.

Pritchard, David. (2002). "Newspaper and Television Stations: A Study of News Coverage of the 2000 Presidential Campaign." Federal Communications Commission, Media Ownership Working Group.

Putnam, Robert. (1995). "Bowling Alone: America's Declining Social Capital." *Journal of Democracy* 6 (1): 65–78.

———. (2000). *Bowling Alone: The Collapse and Revival of American Community*. New York: Simon and Schuster.

Quandt, Thorsten, and Jane Singer. (2009). "Convergence and Cross-Platform Content." In K. Wahl-Jorgensen and T. Hanitzsch (eds.). *The Handbook of Journalism Studies*. New York/London: Routledge, 130–144.

Quinn, Stephen. (2004). "An Intersection of Ideals: Journalism, Profits, Technology and Convergence." *Convergence* 10 (4): 109–123.

Raboy, Marc. (1990). *Missed Opportunities: The Story of Canada's Broadcasting Policy*. Montreal: McGill-Queen's University Press.

Reuters. (2009, Oct. 2). "Content sharing." *The Globe and Mail*, B4.

Robertson, Grant. (2009, Oct. 30). "National Post to rejoin chain of papers." *The Globe and Mail*, B1.

———. (2010, Nov.). "28/01/2008 the day Leonard Asper lost Bay Street." *Report on Business: The Globe and Mail*, 34–45.

Robertson, Grant, and Susan Krashinsky. (2010, May 11). "With salesman's touch, Godfrey claims CanWest." *The Globe and Mail*, A1.

Robertson, Grant, and Andrew Willis. (2009, Oct. 7). "The Asper dream ends, the sell-off begins." *The Globe and Mail*, A1.

Robinson, Piers. (2002). *The CNN Effect: The Myth of News, Foreign Policy and Intervention*. New York: Routledge.

Rogers, Everett. (1962). *Diffusion of Innovations*. New York: The Free Press.

Rogers, Everett, and James Dearing. (1988). "Agenda-Setting Research: Where Has It Been, Where Is It Going?" In J. Anderson (ed.). *Communication Yearbook, Vol. 11*. Beverly Hills, CA: Sage, 68–84.

Romanow, Walter, and Walter Soderlund. (1996). *Media Canada: An Introductory Analysis*. 2nd ed. Toronto: Copp Clark.

Rosenstiel, Tom, and Amy Mitchell. (2003). "Does ownership matter in local television news: A five-year study of ownership and quality." Project for Excellence in Journalism, updated April 29. Retrieved July 15, 2010, from http://www.journalism.org/node/243.

Salwen, Michael. (1988). "Effects of Accumulation of Coverage on Issue Salience in Agenda-Setting." *Journalism Quarterly* 65 (2): 100–106, 130.

Sands, Ken. (2004, May 17). "Struggling with how to teach convergence." Retrieved July 15, 2010, from http://poynteronline.org/column.asp?id=56&aid=657754.

Sauvageau, Florian. (2003). "Convergence, concentration et diversité des médias: mythes et réalités." In M. Venne, dir., *Annuaire du Québec 2004*. Montréal: Fides, 557–564.

Schaffner, Brian, and Michael Wagner. (2006). "Media Deregulation and Local Television Coverage of Senate Campaigns." Paper presented at the annual meeting of the American Political Science Association, Philadelphia, PA.

Scheufele, Dietram, and David Tewksbury. (2007). "Framing, Agenda-Setting and Priming: The Evolution of Three Media Effects Models." *Journal of Communication* 57: 9–20.

Schiller, Herbert. (1973). *The Mind Managers*. Boston: Beacon Press.

Scott, Ben. (2005). "A Contemporary History of Digital Journalism." *Television and New Media* 6 (1): 89–126.

Shade, Leslie Regan. (2005). "Aspergate: Concentration, Convergence, and Censorship in Canadian Media." In David Skinner, James Compton, and Michael Gasher (eds.). *Converging Media, Diverging Politics: A Political Economy of News Media in the United States and Canada*. Toronto: Rowman & Littlefield, 101–116.

Shaw, Donald, and Bradley Hamm. (1997). "Agendas for a Public Union or for Private Communities: How Individuals Are Using Media to Reshape American Society." In M. McCombs, D. Shaw, and D. Weaver (eds.). *Communication and Democracy: Exploring the Intellectual Frontiers in Agenda-Setting Theory.* Mahwah, NJ: Lawrence Erlbaum Associates, 209–230.

Shoemaker, Pamela, and Stephen Reese. (1991, 2nd ed. 1996). *Mediating the Message: Theories of Influences on Mass Media Content.* White Plains, NY: Longmans.

Siebert, Fred, Theodore Peterson, and Wilbur Schramm. (1956). *Four Theories of the Press: The Authoritarian, Libertarian, Social Responsibility and Soviet Communist Concepts of the What the Press Should Be and Do.* Urbana: University of Illinois Press.

Siegel, Arthur. (1983). *Politics and the Media in Canada.* Toronto: McGraw-Hill Ryerson.

Silcock, B. William, and Susan Keith. (2006). "Translating the Tower of Babel? Issues of Definition, Language, and Culture in Converged Newsrooms." *Journalism Studies* 7 (4): 610–627.

Simone, Maria, and Jan Fernback. (2006). "Invisible Hands or Public Spheres? Theoretical Foundations for U.S. Broadcast Policy." *Communication Law and Policy* 11 (2): 287–313.

Singer, Jane. (2004a). "Strange Bedfellows? The Diffusion of Convergence in Four News Organizations." *Journalism Studies* 5 (3): 3–38.

———. (2004b). "More than Ink-Stained Wretches: The Resocialization of Print Journalists in Converged Newsrooms." *Journalism & Mass Communication Quarterly* 81 (4): 838–856.

Skinner, David, and Mike Gasher. (2005). "So Much by So Few: Media Policy and Ownership in Canada." In David Skinner, James Compton, and Michael Gasher (eds.). *Converging Media, Diverging Politics: A Political Economy of News Media in the United States and Canada.* Toronto: Rowman & Littlefield, 51–76.

Smith, Laura, Andrea Tanner, and Sonya Forte Duhé. (2007). "Convergence Concerns in Local Television: Conflicting Views from the Newsroom." *Journal of Broadcasting and Electronic Media* 51 (4): 555–574.

Soderlund, Walter, and Kai Hildebrandt. (2005). *Canadian Newspaper Ownership in the Era of Convergence: Rediscovering Social Responsibility.* Edmonton: University of Alberta Press.

Sonnac, Nathalie. (2009). "L'économie de la presse: vers un nouveau modèle d'affaires?" *Les Cahiers du journalisme* 20: 22–49.

Soroka, Stuart, and Patrick Fournier. (2003, Feb. 11). "Survey Results: Newspapers in Canada Pilot Study." Paper presented at the conference, "Who Controls Canada's Media?" McGill University.

Soupcoff, Marni. (2004, Oct.). "Could Less Be More? The Truth About Media Consolidation and Concentration." *Fraser Forum*, 8–10.

Sparks, Robert, Mary Lynn Young, and Simon Darnell. (2006). "Convergence, Corporate Restructuring, and Canadian Online News, 2000–2003." *Canadian Journal of Communication* 31 (2): 391–423.

Statistics Canada. (2003). *Canada's Journey to an Information Society*. Retrieved July 15, 2010, from http://www.statcan.gc.ca/pub/56-508-x/pdf/4200142-eng.pdf.

———. (2010). "Canadian Internet Use Survey." Retrieved July 15, 2010, from http://www.statcan.gc.ca/daily/quotidien/100510/dq100510a-eng.htm.

Steuter, Erin. (1999). "The Irvings Cover Themselves: Media Representations of the Irving Oil Refinery Strike, 1994–96." *Canadian Journal of Communication* 24 (4): 629–647.

Sturgeon, Jamie. (2010, July 2). "Media chain to be called Postmedia Network." *Financial Times*. Retrieved July 7, 2010, from http://www.financialpost.com/news/media+chain+called+Postmedia+Network/3229434/story.

Sutcliffe, John, Walter Soderlund, Martha Lee, and Kai Hildebrandt. (2009). "The Reporting of International News in Canada: Continuity and Change, 1988–2006." *American Review of Canadian Studies* 39 (2): 131–146.

Taras, David. (2001, 2nd ed. 2005). *Power and Betrayal in the Canadian Media*. Peterborough, ON: Broadview Press.

Toronto Sun Family: 1971–2010. (2009, Aug. 21). "CP vs Sun Media." Retrieved July 15, 2010, from http://torontosunfamily.blogspot.com/2009/08/cp-vs-sun-media.html.

Trichur, Rita. (2006, June 29). "CanWest serves notice to leave CP; national news service would continue: publisher says it's keeping options open." *Toronto Star* [ON Edition]. Retrieved June 29, 2008, from http://www.proquest.com.ezproxy.uwindsor.ca.

Van Dijk, Teun. (1988). "How 'They' Hit the Headlines: Ethnic Minorities in the Press." In G. Smitherman-Donaldson and T. Van Dijk (eds.). *Discourse and Discrimination*. Detroit: Wayne State University Press, 221–262.

Waddell, Christopher. (2009, June 16–20). "The Future for the Canadian Media." *Policy Options*.

Weaver, David. (2007). "Thoughts on Agenda Setting, Framing, and Priming." *Journal of Communication* 57 (1): 142–147.

Wendland, Mike. (2001, Feb. 21). "Newspaper, TV stations and web sites converge to create a new media entity—a news factory." *Detroit Free Press*, E1.

Willis, Andrew. (2009, Oct. 2). "Godfrey wins buyers for buyout of CanWest papers." *The Globe and Mail*, B1.

———. (2009, Oct. 8). "Scotiabank, creditors to control CanWest dailies." *The Globe and Mail*, B1.

Windsor Star. (2008, Feb. 21). "CBC initiates shakeup." *The Windsor Star*, B1.

Winseck, Dwayne. (2008). "The State of Media Ownership and Media Markets: Competition or Concentration and Why Should We Care?" *Sociology Compass* 2 (1): 34–47.

Winter, James. (2002, May/June). "Canada's Media Monopoly." *Extra!* Retrieved July 15, 2010, from http://www.fair.org/index.php?page=1106.

Wolfsfeld, Gadi. (1997). *Media and Political Conflict: News from the Middle East*. Cambridge: Cambridge University Press.

———. (2004). *Media and the Path to Peace*. Cambridge: Cambridge University Press.

World Press Freedom Committee. (1981). *Declaration of Talloires: A Constructive Approach to a Global Information Order*. Retrieved July 15, 2010, from http://www.wpfc.org/DeclarationofTalloires.html.

Worsfold, P.J. (2007, Mar. 14). *Case Study: Special Senate Committee on Mass Media & the Royal Commission on Newspapers*. Retrieved May 7, 2010, from http://www.cruxstrategies.com/content.case-study.

Contributors

WALTER SODERLUND (PHD, University of Michigan, 1970) is Professor Emeritus in the Department of Political Science at the University of Windsor. He began studying the impact of media ownership in Canada in the context of the 1972 federal election and has maintained an ongoing interest in the topic. In addition to co-authoring *Media Canada* (1996) with Walt Romanow, he collaborated with Kai Hildebrandt on *Canadian Newspaper Ownership in the Era of Convergence* (2005), a study of the impact of Conrad Black's ownership influence. Since retirement in 2002, his primary research focus has been on the relationship between media coverage of humanitarian crises and international intervention. Publications in this area include *Humanitarian Crises and Intervention* (2008) and *The Responsibility to Protect in Darfur* (2010). He is currently working on media coverage of the conflict in the Congo.

COLETTE BRIN (PHD, Université Laval, 2002) is Professor in the Département d'information et de communication at Université Laval. A former journalist at Radio-Canada, her work focuses on the changing conditions and practices of journalism, more specifically on the adaptation of newsroom structures and routines. She is co-author of *Nature et transformations du journalisme* (2004).

LYDIA MILJAN (PHD, University of Calgary, 2000) is Associate Professor in the Department of Political Science at the University of Windsor. She teaches in the areas of Canadian public policy, research methodology, and politics and the media. Her main research interests include how journalists' personal views are reflected in news content, and public opinion formation. She has published two books, *Public Policy in Canada* (forthcoming, 2012), and *Hidden Agendas: How Journalists Influence the News* (2004), with Barry Cooper. *Hidden Agendas* was short-listed for the Donner Prize for the best book in public policy in 2003–2004.

KAI HILDEBRANDT (PHD, University of Michigan, 1990) is Associate Professor Emeritus in the Department of Communication, Media and Film at the University of Windsor. An expert in the application of quantitative research methods, he is co-author of *Germany Transformed* (1991), and *Humanitarian Crises and Intervention* (2008). He is also co-editor of *Television Advertising in Canadian Elections* (1999) and collaborated on *Canadian Newspaper Ownership in the Era of Convergence* (2005), with Walter Soderlund.

Index

accountability, 12
advertising, 70, 72, 80, 81, 91, 99, 110n7
Agence France-Presse, 71
agenda setting, 3
Aird Commission, 10
Akin, David, 79–81
Alberta Press Council, 107
all-news channels, 32, 106, 107, 117n1
arts coverage, 83, 86
Asper family, 25, 103
Asper, Leonard, 26–27
The Associated Press, 16
audiences, 6, 15, 70, 71, 72
audio content, 74

bankruptcies, 103–04
BCE. *See* Bell Canada Enterprises
Bell Canada Enterprises, 1, 41, 74, 99, 104, 109n2
Bell Globemedia, 1, 15–16, 34, 105–06, 109n2
blogs, 90
breaking news, 3–4, 71, 72, 73, 100
broadcasting, 5, 10–11, 34, 74
    See also public broadcasting; radio; television
Broadcasting Act, 10
Bryce Commission, 10

Bushnell Communications, 10
business models
    conventional, 68, 70, 72, 79–82
    new, 81, 88–89, 98–99
    vertical integration, 74

Canada Newspaper Act (proposed), 11
Canadian Broadcasting Commission, 10
Canadian Media Guild, 12
Canadian National Railways, 9
The Canadian Press
    and content similarity, 44–45, 51–52, 56
    and corporate news services, 68, 89
    for cost-sharing, 16
    departures from, 70, 72, 73, 85, 92, 110n8, 112n2, 113n1, 114n4
    finances, 115n2
    future of, 70, 72, 92, 94, 101
    role of, 101
    vs. QMI, 76–77, 85
Canadian Radio Broadcasting Commission, 10
Canadian Radio-television and Telecommunications Commission

on concentration of information, 75
on cross-ownership, 21–23, 88
interference with, 106
on media concentration, 22, 96–97
on news coverage by converged media, 35
on separate newsrooms, 83, 111n3
signal fees, 114n5
television networks buying local newspapers, 34
testimony to Senate committee, 7
Canwest
adoption of convergence, 57
bankruptcy, ix, 100–01, 115n1
content sharing, 72–73, 96
on convergence, 26–27
corporate news service, 70
job satisfaction, 14
national editorials, 24, 25
story similarities, 55
Canwest Global Communications, 1, 8, 14, 15, 34, 41, 47–48, 103–04
Canwest Interactive, 27
Canwest News Service, 70, 72, 73, 89, 94, 112n2, 114n2
carriage and content, 99, 104
CBC, 23, 33–34, 56, 82
See also Radio-Canada
censorship, 9, 12
Chronicle-Herald, 2
citizen journalists, 90, 92, 100
civic disengagement, 4
classified advertising, 72
cloning, 28
Cohen, Bernard, 3
commentary-talk news, 87
Commission de la culture, 12
communities, 4–5, 101
concentration, 74–75, 83–84

Confédération des syndicats nationaux, 107
content
consumer-controlled, 89
cost of, 16, 89
creating, 68–69
cross-media, 23, 73–74, 98, 100
differentiation, 73–74, 76, 97
distribution, 41, 68–69, 88, 104
exclusive, 76
importance of, 35–36
influences on, 30–31
local, 24–25, 73
and media impact, 5–6
and organizational structure, 26
owner-controlled, 6, 8–9, 12, 32
synergy, 74
television-generated, 71–72
vs. ratings, 82
See also online products
content diversity
and corporate news services, 76–77, 92
and democracy, 4
effect of convergence on, 12, 13, 43–48, 83, 86, 97
effect on conventional media, 89
maintaining, 9, 85–86, 101
content sharing
among journalists, 72–73
and corporate news services, 68, 71
for cost savings, 70, 90, 91
defined, 29
evidence of, 14, 49–50, 95–98
future of, 76, 97–98, 116n1
impediments to, 82, 89
justification for, 14
labour on, 93–94
outcome of, x, 95–96
owners against, 96

as purpose of convergence, 6
regulators' view of, 89–92
software for, 27
between television and
 newspapers, x
trends opposing, 76
union negotiations, 86
vs. differentiation, 97
See also stories
content similarity, 43–52, 62–64
See also stories
conventional media, 27–28, 67, 69–75, 88–89, 96–97, 111n10
convergence
 achieving, 34–35, 95–96, 100–02
 advantages and disadvantages of, 2, 6, 7, 12–13, 33–35, 86, 110n7
 background to, 21–24
 and content diversity, 12, 13
 continuum of types of, 28, 29
 for cost saving, 16, 26, 28, 69, 76
 defined, 6, 25–26, 27, 29
 and democracy, 2, 17, 69, 74–75
 evolution of, 31
 first age of, 104
 future of, 97, 100–02, 105–06
 horizontal, 104
 impediments to, 31, 75–76
 "kings of", 105
 in local media, 57, 62
 original content, 69
 purpose of, 6, 15, 69, 76
 reputation of, 76
 results of, ix, 95–96
 second age of, 97, 104, 105
 success factors, 29–30
 2.0, 97, 104, 105
 vertical, 74, 97, 99, 104
 vs. concentration, 83–84

See also cross-ownership; regulations
coopetition, 28, 32–33, 42, 58
corporate news services
 and content diversity, 85, 92
 and content sharing, 68, 71, 72, 86, 89, 94, 97–98
 for cost saving, 70, 94
 effects of, 101
 future of, 74, 89, 92, 94, 100–01, 112n2
 operations of, 76–77
 Quebec, 68, 76–77, 85
 for website content, 73
cost saving, 26, 28, 30, 69, 70, 94, 98
CRBC, 10
credibility of media, 13–14
cross-ownership, 13, 41, 42, 74–75, 88
cross-promotion, 28, 32–33, 41–42, 56, 83, 86
CRTC. *See* Canadian Radio-television and Telecommunications Commission
CTV, 1, 2, 32, 99
CTVglobemedia
 acquisition of the *Toronto Star*, 17
 breakup of, 15
 content assets, 41
 content sharing, 14
 creation of, 28, 34, 105–06
 editorial direction, 47
 fragment reaggregration, 16
 move to convergence, 33, 104
cultural criticism school, 23
culture, 9, 26
See also journalists

Dalfen, Charles, 7
Davey Senate Committee, 8, 10–11
Davey, Keith, 11

democracy
   and a free press, 2–3
   and audience fragmentation, 6
   and convergence, 2, 17, 69, 74–75, 102
   and diverse points of view, 4–7
   media's role, 5–6
   and niche media, 5
   and political polarization of media, 107
Desmarais family, 84
digital technology. *See* new media
disaggregation, 15

economic crisis. *See* financial crisis
economies of scale, 15–16, 21, 76
editorial policy, 8, 14, 15
editorial voices, 22
editorials
   future of, 74
   national, 24–25
   owners' influence on, 8, 22, 47, 50, 91
   spin, 47–48, 49, 52–53, 54, 60, 61, 75
Edmonton, 57–64
election coverage, 113n4, 116n1, 116n2
"The Enduring Newspaper", 79–81
English-language media, 12, 43–50, 69, 106
entertainment coverage, 26, 83, 86, 97

Fédération professionelle des journalistes du Québec, 12
"fee for carriage", 74, 114n5, 117n5
Field, Terry, 81–82
Final Report on the Canadian News Media, 2–3, 92
financial crisis, x, 67, 80, 84, 90, 91, 105
framing, 3
free press, 2, 12

French-language media, 1, 44–50, 69
   See also Quebec; Radio-Canada

gatekeeping, 4
Gesca, 14, 32, 34, 69, 74–75, 86, 98, 99, 109n3
Globe and Mail, 32, 33, 106
government, 12, 84–85, 87, 89–92, 106
   See also public broadcasting; regulations

Hollinger Inc., 1, 103–04
homogenization, 84, 85–86, 101
human-interest stories, 63

information
   choice of sources, 13
   concentration of, 74–75, 84
   as content, 23
   convergence of, 26
   and democracy, 6
   digital dissemination, 27
   personal sources of, 4–5, 7
   quality of, 98
   sharing vs. controlling, 35
innovation, 7
international news, 51, 54, 55, 56, 101
Internet
   advertisers on, 70
   attention on, x
   audiences, 100
   cross-promotion of online products, 56, 73
   future of, 105
   and individual choice, 4
   news on, 71, 86, 100, 110n10
   takeover of advertising, 28
   writing for, 94
   See also new media; online products

Irving family, 11
Irving newspapers, 24

job cuts, 69, 77, 80, 82–88, 91, 93, 98, 107
journalism
   convergence in, 27, 82
   culture of, 31, 34–35, 68–70, 82, 85, 86, 91, 96, 98
   education, 92–93, 100
   freedom and integrity, 24–25, 91
   future of, 74, 77, 93, 97, 100
   online, 94
   paying for, 81, 89
   professionalism of, 92, 100
   public good of, 82
   quality of, 30, 70, 84, 87–88, 90, 97
   and risk, 92
   tabloid-style, 50–51
   television, 82
   See also pack journalism
journalists
   adjusting to convergence, 34, 84–86
   citizen, 90, 91, 100
   in converged work environments, 29, 74
   cost of, 16
   on cross-ownership, 79–87
   on editorial independence, 14
   education of, 93, 100
   and the free press, 12
   goals of, 31
   in-house vs. external, 34
   informal content sharing, 72–73
   interpreting events, 3
   interviewing other journalists, 32, 33, 34, 82
   job cuts, 69, 77, 80, 82–84, 87, 88, 91, 93, 98, 107
   job satisfaction, 14
   multitasking, 12–13, 27, 32, 34–35, 74, 77, 80, 93–94, 96, 100, 115n3, 116n2
   newspaper, 31, 32
   owners' control of, 23–24, 48
   political leanings, 86
   radio, 99
   resistance to convergence, 31, 68, 82–83, 84–85
   self-censorship, 9, 12
   sharing content, 72
   skills, 32, 80, 97, 98, 100
   television, 31, 32, 82, 97
   training, 34

Kent Commission. *See* Royal Commission on Newspapers
Kent, Thomas, 11

La Presse, 2, 32, 84, 90, 98, 99
labour
   conflicts, 34, 85, 91, 107
   on content sharing, 93–94
   negotiations, 86, 91, 94, 96, 107
   research by, 34
   workload, 94
   See also job cuts; unions
Lareau, Lise, 12–13, 93–94, 101, 115n4
Latendresse, Richard, 84–85
layoffs, 69, 77, 80, 82–88, 91, 93
Le Devoir, 2
Le Journal de Montréal, 69, 83–85, 90, 91, 107
Le Soleil, 2
Libertarian Theory, 2
local media, 14, 57–64

marginalized groups, 15
mass media, 3, 4–5, 6, 9–14, 10–11, 15

See also media
media outlets, quantity of, 6-8
media ownership convergence. See convergence
Merrill, John, 92-93
Mike Duffy (television program), 32-33, 111n2
mobile devices, 104
Monty, Jean, 105
multimedia, 73-74
    See also online products
Murdoch, Rupert, 81

narrowcasting, 2
national agenda, 101
national community, 4-5
National Guild of Canadian Media, 14
national news, 51, 54, 55, 101
National Post, 103-04, 117n5
new media
    competition from, x
    convergence in, 27
    effects on conventional media, 67, 97
    smartphones, 105
    as source of information, 6
    vs. conventional media, 88-89, 97
    See also technology
New York Times news service, 71
New York Times website, 7
news
    all-news channels, 32, 106, 107, 117n1
    amount in newspapers, 85-86
    commentary-talk, 87
    commodity vs. exclusive, 76
    complex, 93
    cost of gathering, 16
    coverage, 30, 69
    cross-ownership effects, 13, 93-94
    interest in, 72
    local, 30, 73, 75, 76, 91
    news brand, 91
    owners influencing, 4
    paying for, 81-82, 91
    political polarization, 107
    public affairs, 24
    quality of, 30, 70, 84, 87-88, 90, 93-94, 97, 98, 99
    sources of, 17
    television, 17, 73, 82
    See also breaking news
news bureaus, 98
news services. See corporate news services; wire services
newspapers
    advertising, 28, 72, 80, 81
    audiences, 70, 72
    business model, 68, 70, 72, 79-82, 86, 98-99
    circulation, 80, 81, 89
    credibility of, 13-14
    financial crisis, 84
    future of, 67, 69-72, 79-82, 91-92, 99-100, 107
    inserts, 81
    journalism, 31, 32, 97
    local, 22-23, 34, 86, 109n3
    local stories, 14
    national chains, 17
    news quantity, 85-86
    as news source, 17, 86
    online, 7, 23, 69-70, 72, 81-82, 89, 97, 100
    profitability, 6, 84, 86, 89
    and radio broadcasting, 9, 10-11
    readership, 81, 87, 110n10
    and television, 28, 68, 73-74, 104
newsrooms
    culture of, 31, 69-70

independence of, 83, 84
research on, 26
restructuring of, 90
separation of, 96, 111n3
shared, 29, 99, 107
See also job cuts
newswires. *See* wire services
niche media, 5

old media. *See* conventional media
online products
    advertising, 70
    as conventional media
        supplement, 110n10
    corporate news services, 73
    newspapers, 73, 81, 89, 97, 100
    profitability, 68, 70, 71, 73, 81, 89,
        100
    television, 73, 90, 97, 99
    theft of, 81–82
    video, 105
    writing for, 94
opinions. *See* editorials; points of view
owners
    concentration of, 11, 12
    content control, 4, 6, 8–9, 12, 83
    content sharing, 96
    and editorial direction, 47, 50,
        88, 91
    goals, 8
    and government, 84
    journalism control, 23–24, 48, 83
    public, 10
    regulation of, 10–11
    relationships with government, 84
ownership concentration, 14–17, 21

pack journalism, 50, 51–52, 58, 85
Page, Benjamin, 16
Péladeau, Pierre Karl, 83–84, 107

photographers, 31
pipes, 41, 99, 104, 106
points of view
    alternative, 97
    convergence affecting, 7, 12–13, 14,
        23, 25
    and democracy, 4–7
    local, 14, 75
political communities, 4, 101
politics
    coverage of, 85, 87, 90, 111n2, 113n4,
        114n3
    media influence over, 74–75, 106
    polarization of media, 107
Postmedia Network Canada Corp.,
    104
Power Corporation, 2, 10, 109n3
press associations, 92, 107
press conferences, 50, 51–52, 56, 71
Press Council, 12
Press Ownership Review Board, 11
press releases, 50, 51–52, 55, 56
programming, 23
public affairs coverage, 24
public broadcasting, 10, 75, 82, 90,
    99, 109n6
public interest, 22
public interest values, 24–25
public opinion, 3, 13–14, 15
public ownership, 10
public policy, 3, 8–9

QMI. *See* Quebec Media Inc.
Quebec
    content diversity, 75–76
    content sharing, 75–76, 85, 91
    convergence, 90–93
    democracy, 74–75, 102
    financial crisis, 84

geographic concentration of news coverage, 42
government regulations, 69, 92
journalism, 82–87, 92, 96
local news, 91, 109n3
media ownership, 12
ownership concentration, 12
provincial vs. national news focus, 43
television, 87
See also French-language media; Quebec Media Inc.
Quebec Media Inc., 68, 69, 76–77, 85, 89, 97, 115n4
Quebec National Assembly, 85, 90, 114n3
Quebec Press Council, 90, 107
Quebecor
business model, 76, 83–84
content assets, 41
content sharing, x, 69, 75–76, 86
convergence, 85, 96–97
corporate news service, 68
cross-promotion of entertainment, 83, 86
and democracy, 102
editorials, 75–76
English-language market, 106
fragment reaggregration, 16
Groupe Vidéotron Ltée, 1, 104
integrating media types, 41
interference in government, 106
job satisfaction, 14
newsrooms, 34, 75–76, 83, 96, 111n3
ownership of broadcasters and newspapers, 28
vertical integration, 74, 104

Rabinovitch, Robert, 23
radio, 9–10, 22–23, 56, 90, 99

Radio-Canada, 14, 32, 34, 69, 74–75, 90, 99
See also CBC
reaggregation, 1, 15, 16
recession. *See* financial crisis
regulations
consolidation permission, 28
and convergence, 21, 22–23, 96–97
editorial voices, 22
impeding convergence, 68, 69, 83
newsroom separation, 75–76, 83
ownership, 10–11, 88
United States, 111n1
Report of the Royal Commission on Corporate Concentration, 10
Reuters, 71, 105
Rogers Communications, 10, 13, 41
Royal Commission on Newspapers, 8, 10–11, 24
Royal Commission on Radio Broadcasting, 10
Rue Frontenac, 107

Sabia, Michael, 105
Saint-Jean, Armande, 12, 13
scrums, 56
second-level agenda setting, 3
Shaw Communications, 41, 104
smartphones, 105
social capital, 4
social media, 99
software for content sharing, 27
sources, 46–47, 62–63, 75, 82, 85, 90
See also corporate news services; stories; wire services
Southam group, 11
Special Senate Committee on Mass Media, 8, 10–11
spin. *See* editorials

Standing Senate Committee on Transport and Communications, 2–3, 7, 12, 21, 22, 92
state. *See* government
stories
    dimensions, 44, 45, 52, 54, 59
    language, 45–46, 59, 62
    leads, 43–44, 52, 58–59, 62
    similarity, 42, 55–56, 60–63
    sources, 46–47, 53, 54, 60, 62, 82
Sun Media, 28
SunTVNews, 106
Syndicat des communications de Radio-Canada, 34
synergies, ix, 74, 98

tabloids, 50–51
technology, 23, 26, 74
    See also new media
television
    business models, 68, 89, 98–99
    cable, 4, 74, 88, 99, 104, 114n5, 117n5
    consolidation of ownership, 28
    content generation, 71–72
    content sharing impediments, 82
    convergence with newspapers, 68, 73–74, 104
    cross-promotion, 73
    distribution, 4, 88
    "fee for carriage", 74
    French-language, 1
    future of, 67, 69, 74, 82, 99, 105
    and individual choice, 4
    journalism, 31, 32, 82, 97
    local, 22–23, 73, 74, 99
    news, 17, 73, 82, 87
    online, 23, 69, 72, 73, 90, 97, 99
    satellite, 4, 74, 88, 99

specialty channels, 89, 99
Télévision Quatre Saisons, 87, 109n1
Telus, 104
Teneycke, Kory, 106
Thomson, David, 105
Thomson family, 11, 105, 106
Thomson, Roy, 8
Toronto Star, 17, 106
Torstar, 2, 15–16, 106, 110n9
traditional media. *See* conventional media
transparency, 12
trust in media, 13–14
TVA, 83–85, 90, 91, 109n1

unions
    convergence impediments, 4, 68, 69, 83, 96, 107
    negotiations on content sharing, 86
    public broadcasting, 34
    See also labour
United States
    convergence in, 7, 96, 99, 104
    economy, 80, 81
    journalism educators, 92–93
    media intrusions from, 9–10
    newsroom sharing, 29–30
    owners' influence on content, 24
    regulations, 111n1

vertical integration, 74, 97, 99, 104
video, 31, 73, 74, 82, 105–06
Vidéotron, 1, 104
viewpoints. *See* points of view
Voices of Freedom conference, 2
voter attitudes, 3

"War on Terror", 3–4
web applications, attention on, x

websites. *See* Internet; online products
Who Controls Canada's Media, 13
Winnipeg Free Press, 2
wire services
   content sharing, 73
   and content similarity, 50, 51–52, 55, 56
   and editorial similarity, 47
   future of, 74, 94
   newspapers contributing content to, 70, 71
   role of, 16, 74
   See also corporate news services
wireless networks, 104, 105, 106

ZenithOptimedia Canada, 80

Other Titles from The University of Alberta Press

Canadian Newspaper Ownership in the Era of Convergence
Rediscovering Social Responsibility
Walter C. Soderlund, Kai Hildebrandt,
Walter I. Romanow & Ronald H. Wagenberg

216 pages | Tables, bibliography, index
978-0-88864-439-8 | $34.95 (S) paper
Media/Communications

In the News, 2nd edition
The Practice of Media Relations in Canada
William Wray Carney

292 pages | Notes, bibliography
978-0-88864-495-4 | $26.95 (T) paper
Media/Communications

CTV—*The Network That Means Business*
Michael Nolan

440 pages | B&W photos
978-0-88864-384-1 | $34.95 (T) paper
History/Broadcasting